Something To Brew On

John Ballard Jr.

Published by John Ballard Jr., 2023.

SOMETHING TO BREW ON

First edition. April 6, 2023.

Copyright © 2023 John Ballard Jr..

ISBN: 979-8215554326

Written by John Ballard Jr..

Also by John Ballard Jr.

Something To Brew On

I. Acknowledgments

There are many people that helped this book come to fruition. From my wife, Kristina, who first told me to write a book. Yes, I didn't listen. So, it took Debbie Wilson and my Pastor Matthew Pagels to suggest that I write. To my Pastor, I thank you for being an inspiration to live for God.

My wife also made this trip with me, spending hours reading over what I had written and being an encouragement. My long time Pastor and now Bishop James Whitehead, who spent many years encouraging me and teaching me how to live for God, for that I am eternally grateful. To the many others that have provided support and also experiences that have help form this work. I thank you. Most of all, I thank Jesus for never giving up on me and directing me to salvation through Him. Without Jesus and His direction, this book would have never happened.

II. Introduction

The thoughts scattered throughout this book will be like variations of a cup of coffee. Some will be like a smooth cup with a little creamer and sweetener. Some like a cup of espresso small but stout. Some will be like a strong cup of bitter dark roast made in a drip pot like my daddy used to make it. Either way, they are meant to provoke thought and open our eyes, so to speak. To make us look at something a little bit differently. My hope is that you may dig deeper into some of these thoughts and, in turn, draw closer to God. They you might study and show yourself approved unto God. I would hope that you don't just read this book. What I would like is for you to read this book, then start seeing God in your everyday life.

2Co 1:13 Easy English We are writing to you only things that you yourselves can read and understand. And I hope that you will understand completely.

III. The Handicap of Hearing Impairment

We all know someone that doesn't hear well. You may be that someone. You may often be called or call yourself hard of hearing. I am personally hard of hearing. I know all too well the issues that come from not being able to hear well. I don't watch videos without closed captioning as long as they are available. There are some singers that I really cannot understand because of the pitch of their voice. I have been in a room with someone calling my name, and I don't hear them until they get loud. People that are around me a lot, know if they say something and I just stare at them, it means I didn't hear them. Some people are this way because of bad habits when they were younger. Maybe it was loud music, a loud profession, or other loud hobbies without hearing protection. Some of it may be genetic. For some it may even be a combination of the two. Either way, you learn ways to adapt. It may be reading closed captioning or text. It may be reading lips. I once knew someone that said that they couldn't hear, but they could feel their kids moving through the house. So, you may feel. You may use hearing aids. You do what you can to adapt. This can also be referenced to hearing from God. If you can't seem to hear from God then read His text, the Word of God. Feel after God. If you have things that are affecting your hearing from God; tune them out, turn them down or off. Use "hearing aids," go to church and listen to the man of God. Listen to men and women of God in your life. Surround yourself with these types of people. Pray for God to restore your hearing.

Mat 11:15 KJV He that hath ears to hear, let him hear.

Rom 10:14 KJV How then shall they call on him in whom they have not believed? and how shall they believe in him of whom they have not heard? and how shall they hear without a preacher?

IV.

Oftentimes when my children were younger, they may get a splinter that I had to remove. There were also times where I was tossing them in the air, although I always had one hand connected to them, but they didn't realize it. Both of these experiences, along many others, had an aspect of fear that could be attached to it. The fear of pain, the fear of falling, etc. Before I began, I'd tell them "Trust me." As their earthly father, I always tried to do what was best for them, even if it may not have seemed like it to them at the time. Our heavenly Father also wants what is best for us. If we trust in God's word. If we believe that the Word of God is the truth. If we believe that God created the heavens and the earth. If we believe that Jesus was born of a virgin. If we believe that Jesus was beaten for us and died for our sins. If we believe that He was resurrected and freely offers us salvation. Then why worry? Trust God. It is repeated over and over in the Word of God to trust Him. He made everything He can handle your situation, just give it to Him. The Bible states that all things work together for the good of those that love God and are called to his purpose. God, our heavenly Father, is doing what is best for his children, even if sometimes it may not seem like it.

Matthew 7:11 KJV If ye then, being evil, know how to give good gifts unto your children, how much more shall your Father which is in heaven give good things to them that ask him?

V.

You ever drive down the road and see something over in the distance that's just rotting into the ground that you could use. It may be a car, a shed, a tool, or something valuable. It's just sitting there, not getting used, grass growing up around it. It's something that could be utilized, maybe even something that you could utilize. It may be on a piece of property that you can tell nobody's been at in years. Nobody's getting anything out of it, and it just makes you mad. Maybe it is on somebody's property, and it's not getting used. You look at it and can tell they're not gonna get rid of it, but they're not going to use it which also makes you mad. I wonder how many times God looks at us and goes I could use them, I could utilize them, but we're just sitting there letting grass grow around us, not getting used. If God moves on us to use the gift, we draw back and are like no I know I'm not using it, but I don't want anybody else to use it either. We just sit on it. Let us not be like the one talent man. Let's use our gifts.

Mat 5:14-16 KJV 14 Ye are the light of the world. A city that is set on an hill cannot be hid. 15 Neither do men light a candle, and put it under a bushel, but on a candlestick; and it giveth light unto all that are in the house. 16 Let your light so shine before men, that they may see your good works, and glorify your Father which is in heaven.

VI.

The devil is in the details.

How many times have you signed a legal document without reading all of the details? It may have been a vehicle purchase or a home purchase. They present you with countless pages of paperwork. Most of us just skim over it and sign. We don't read all the details. Although what we are signing is something that will affect years of our lives. How about apps for our phones? We find an app we want, and you have to agree to their terms and conditions before you can download the app. What do most people do, click accept. We don't read all the details. Did you know that there are apps that you can download that don't just ask permission for access to things on your phone but also your friends on Facebook and their friends too? You could give access to somebody else's phone that you don't even know by accepting terms and conditions for an app. Which means someone else could do the same to you. You could take every measure to prevent access to things on your phone and your friend's friend on Facebook downloads an app and boom, now somebody has access to your phone. If you had a lawyer read over some of the things we sign, they could advise us or tell us altogether don't sign it. Same with the apps, they may tell us that it is a gross intrusion of privacy.

The thing is we do the same in the spiritual world. We accept details from things that we aren't even aware that we accepted. These things affect our homes and our network of people around us. We watch things and listen to things that affect our spiritual well-being and don't know why we're struggling with things. We don't realize the devil is in the details. He's inserting unwanted stuff into our lives, and we gave him access. We're angry or fighting some temptation that we can't overcome, and we can't seem to put a finger on why. The Bible says we have an advocate with the Father. Jesus is our advocate or lawyer. Now I know he's presenting to the Father which is what a lawyer would do is present your case to someone, but they also give you counsel and legal advice. We can ask Jesus to direct us away from things that we don't need in our lives and direct us towards things we do. Because Jesus knows the details and He knows which way we should go.

1Jn 2:1 KJV My little children, these things write I unto you, that ye sin not. And if any man sin, we have an advocate with the Father, Jesus Christ the righteous:

VII.

Everything cost something. Toilet paper costs money. What we eat and drink. We pay a lot to drive down the road. We finance a vehicle, get insurance on it, then we have to keep putting gas into it, oil changes etc. Yet when it comes to the kingdom of God, we want everything for free. Jesus paid the ultimate price. The early church paid a heavy price. Despite this, we want it for free. We need to turn away from this mentality and be like David. How can I offer to the Lord that which costs me nothing?

2Sa 24:24 ISV "No!" the king replied to Araunah. "I will buy them from you at full price. I won't offer to the LORD my God burnt offerings that cost me nothing." So, David bought the threshing floor and the oxen for 50 silver shekels,

VIII.

Have you ever gotten near a bakery and smell the bread baking? Or maybe you passed a steakhouse, and you could just smell the aroma coming out? These smells had spilled out of the buildings where they were being generated. The outside air was then filled with the smell. Shouldn't we strive to be so full of Christ that it just spills out of us. For out of the abundance of the heart the mouth speaketh. (Matthew 12:34).

Eph 5:1-2 KJV 1 Be ye therefore followers of God, as dear children; 2 And walk in love, as Christ also hath loved us, and hath given himself for us an offering and a sacrifice to God for a sweet-smelling savour.

IX.

I remember one time at one of my jobs, they would provide fruit on ice sometimes during summertime to help cool people off. I was heading to the breakroom for a break, and I just said "Lord, I sure would like some fruit." When I got to the break room there was a cooler of fruit. The thought hit me that God had to have had that working out before I even prayed for it, or it would not have been there when I arrived. Isn't it interesting that God made the heavens and the earth, the fruit trees and everything that grows on the earth? The sun for the day and the moon for the night. The fish, birds, and all other animals. All this before He made man. God always sends the provision for what we need before us. We need not worry.

Phi 4:19 KJV But my God shall supply all your need according to his riches in glory by Christ Jesus.

X.

Falling is going to happen. In the physical world we have gravity constantly pulling us down. Now we need it because it keeps us from floating away. In the spiritual world we have things that pull us down and sometimes we may fall because we lose our balance, or we are carrying too much. Sometimes, though, these things keep us grounded. In the physical sense, it makes no sense to anyone for someone to fall and just stay on the ground. Even if it takes a few minutes, you get back up, you don't just lay there until you die. You might even need help getting up, but you get back up. In the spiritual realm, however, people fall and just stay down. Nobody hardly even gives it any attention. It's not natural to stay down in the physical or the spiritual. Don't stay down, get back up. Even if you fall back down, get back up. Don't lay there and die. Get up and keep moving forward.

Jer 8:4 ISV "You are to say to them, 'This is what the LORD says: "Will a person fall down and then not get up? Will someone turn away and then not turn back again?

Pro 24:16 ISV for though a righteous man falls seven times, he will rise again, but the wicked stumble into calamity.

Mic 7:8 KJV Rejoice not against me, O mine enemy: when I fall, I shall arise; when I sit in darkness, the LORD shall be a light unto me.

XI.

Most of us have known someone that was in an abusive relationship that got out of it, then turned around and went right back. When this happens, we all ask- "Why?" Why would you go back into that kind of relationship? You were mistreated, abused physically and/or emotionally. You escaped! Why would you go back? It all starts with communication; they start communicating with their abuser. Then, before you know it, they are back in the prison they escaped. How many of us get out of the world and start living for God just to turn and start dabbling in the world again. We start communicating with things we should be avoiding. Too many times it results in going back into captivity, to our old lives, and turning our backs on God. The same way the first doesn't make sense the second doesn't either. Make sure we aren't communicating with the wrong things, Draw near to God

Jer 2:11-12 ISV 11 Has a nation ever changed gods when they aren't even gods? But my people have exchanged their glory for that which does not profit. 12 Heavens, be appalled at this, be shocked, be utterly devastated," declares the LORD.

2Pe 2:20-22 KJV 20 For if after they have escaped the pollutions of the world through the knowledge of the Lord and Saviour Jesus Christ, they are again entangled therein, and overcome, the latter end is worse with them than the beginning. 21 For it had been better for them not to have known the way of righteousness, than, after they have known it, to turn from the holy commandment delivered unto them. 22 But it is happened unto them according to the true proverb, The dog is turned to his own vomit again; and the sow that was washed to her wallowing in the mire.

XII.

If you own property on a road front, you probably have to deal with other people's trash. They just drive by and toss their trash in your front yard with no concern for anyone. It is infuriating and disrespectful. We have to get out there and pick it up. Worse yet, if we don't pick it up and later hit it with a mower, it spreads out even more, creating a bigger mess to clean. Our church has the same problem: always trash out front to pick up. It makes a piece of property look less valuable. The thing is though we let people throw trash into our lives, and we don't say anything about it. Most of the time we just leave it there, and it becomes worse and worse. It's about time that we clean up the trash. We need to stop letting people litter our lives with stuff that we don't want and devalues who we really are. We also don't need to let people trash our church in the spiritual realm and clutter it up with things that devalue it.

Heb 12:1 KJV Wherefore seeing we also are compassed about with so great a cloud of witnesses, let us lay aside every weight, and the sin which doth so easily beset us, and let us run with patience the race that is set before us,

John 15:3 BBE You are clean, even now, through the teaching which I have given you.

XIII.

I once worked with a guy that was terrible at spelling. The funny thing about it was that he would ask you how to spell something then tell you that you were wrong. I remember one instance where he asked a coworker how to spell "wand" in "air wand". The coworker told him W-A-N-D, to which he replied that doesn't sound right. So, he spelled it "wond". It doesn't make sense to us to discredit someone's help purposely and knowingly in an area that we are weak. Don't we do this though. We get shown the right way or a better way to do something, but we press on in the way we believe it to be. If someone shows us a different way to get closer to God, we at least should consider it.

Act 18:24-28 KJV 24 And a certain Jew named Apollos, born at Alexandria, an eloquent man, and mighty in the scriptures, came to Ephesus. 25 This man was instructed in the way of the Lord; and being fervent in the spirit, he spake and taught diligently the things of the Lord, knowing only the baptism of John. 26 And he began to speak boldly in the synagogue: whom when Aquila and Priscilla had heard, they took him unto them, and expounded unto him the way of God more perfectly. 27 And when he was disposed to pass into Achaia, the brethren wrote, exhorting the disciples to receive him: who, when he was come, helped them much which had believed through grace: 28 For he mightily convinced the Jews, and that publickly, shewing by the scriptures that Jesus was Christ.

When Apollos was shown a more perfect way he didn't resist. I'm sure that he applied the knowledge that he had and examined what was told to him and followed what had been taught to him. Instead of arguing. I believe Apollos had a strong desire to please God. When he was presented with a deeper understanding. Instead of resisting it, he studied and saw if there might be something that he didn't know. Shouldn't we all be this way. If God has something more for us, shouldn't we follow it?

Act 17:11-12 KJV 11 These were more noble than those in Thessalonica, in that they received the word with all readiness of mind, and searched the scriptures daily, whether those things were so. 12 Therefore many of them believed; also, of honourable women which were Greeks, and of men, not a few.

XIV.

I needed to change the disc brakes on my wife's vehicle. So, I went to the parts store. I got the discs, and the guy behind the counter pulls out that little pack of grease that they always sell you. He started to say something about it, when I kind of cut him off and said, "yeah I'm going to use it." He says, "Well don't put it on the back of the disc. That isn't where it goes. It goes on the guide pins. So, the brakes can move smoothly." I was flabbergasted. I had been told my entire life that they went on the back of the discs, even by parts store workers. How he explained it made perfect sense. You ever had something that you had learned a certain way and had done it that way your entire life. Then, one day you meet someone that shows you a different way of doing it. Sometimes we may be so set in our way of doing it, or it may be because of who taught us. That we won't even consider another way.

What if there was a better way, a different way, of living for God. What if God wanted us to step out of our traditions and what we've always done to step up to a higher level. Would we be so set in our ways that we wouldn't even entertain the idea? Would we lean on that's the way my parents did it, that's the way I've always done it? Remember most of the religious sect when Jesus came, missed Him because it was against their traditions and how they had learned. Let's look here at the disciples of John. They ran into Paul and Paul told them there was something more they needed. They gladly listened. Shouldn't we be glad to listen if someone shows a way to get closer to God. Even if it's not the way we've learned. Let us be sensitive and always be willing to follow God's leading.

Act 19:1-6 KJV 1 And it came to pass, that, while Apollos was at Corinth, Paul having passed through the upper coasts came to Ephesus: and finding certain disciples, 2 He said unto them, Have ye received the Holy Ghost since ye believed? And they said unto him, We have not so much as heard whether there be any Holy Ghost. 3 And he said unto them, Unto what then were ye baptized? And they said, Unto John's baptism. 4 Then said Paul, John verily baptized with the baptism of repentance, saying unto the people, that they should believe on him which should come after him, that is, on Christ Jesus. 5 When they heard this, they were baptized in the name of the Lord Jesus. 6 And when Paul had laid his hands upon them, the Holy Ghost came on them; and they spake with tongues, and prophesied.

XV.

Have you ever been fishing on a lake that you drive by often? You get out in the water and start looking around because you don't recognize where you are. You're not lost, you just don't recognize where you are. Then you realize, oh that's where I am. You are looking at the back side of houses that you normally see from the front. You're looking at the road you normally drive from a different point of view. Sometimes we may feel that way in our life with God. We may feel lost because we don't recognize where we are. Like standing in a boat on the water we may feel unstable or like we can't move much. All the time God may have us in a place that we've never been before to show us a new angle or perspective. We have to be patient and just keep on fishing. Soon enough everything will become clear.

"Trust in the LORD with all thine heart; and lean not unto thine own understanding. In all thy ways acknowledge him, and he shall direct thy paths." Pro 3: 5-6.

XVI.

I have heard and read many stories about people living near each other for years and not knowing that they were related. One or both may have been adopted and come to find out that they are siblings. It may have been that they had such a large family that they didn't realize they were cousins. These people may have been best friends but didn't really know who the other person was. I think this can apply to our relationship with Jesus. We can go to church faithfully. We can love Jesus and yet not really know Him. Let us move closer to really knowing Jesus.

Joh 14:9 ISV "Have I been with you all this time, Philip, and you still do not know me?" Jesus asked him. "The person who has seen me has seen the Father. So how can you say, 'Show us the Father'?

XVII.

You ever get cut off in traffic and suddenly it reveals something in you that needs to go? Maybe it's deeper than that. Maybe someone hurt you. I mean really hurt you, and they were legitimately wrong. Now something is revealed or brought to life in you that you didn't know was in you.

The betrayal of Judas is known throughout the world. The name Judas is associated with betrayal. Nobody likes a "Judas" or someone that betrays you. What if though our Judas causes us to crucify something in ourselves. What if something has to die in us to make us more like Jesus. It may be a person or a situation but if it makes us more like Jesus, we should be thankful for that, even though we may not be thankful for the Judas, the person that hurt us, the one that cut us off in traffic, the one that cheated us, but we can be thankful for the results.

1 Thessalonians 5:18 KJV In every thing give thanks: for this is the will of God in Christ Jesus concerning you.

XVIII.

Have you ever decided to clean your property up of overgrowth, vines, and weeds? If you live in Louisiana, mimosa trees and thistles. You get it cleaned up, and it looks great. You keep up with the mowing and weed eating. You don't realize that the stuff you cut down is slowly coming back. Then one day boom, you're like when did that happen? The vines are back, the weeds are rapidly growing, and the mimosa trees are back with even more appearing. What happened? You were doing what you thought was right, mowing and weed eating. The thing is you have to stay attentive and not just do the normal things. You have to go the extra mile and work a little more to keep the overgrowth at bay. If at any time you let your guard down, then it will all come back and then some. The thing is it's the same with our spiritual walk with God. We decide to clean things out of our lives and live for God more fervently. We start off good, we pray more, we stop listening to and watching things that distract us from our walk with God. We feel God more, we see His hand at work in our lives. Then slowly we let our guard down and boom, we're worse off than we were before. Little things creep in and choke out our walk.

We have to live for God on purpose and with purpose.

Mat 13:22-23 KJV 22 He also that received seed among the thorns is he that heareth the word; and the care of this world, and the deceitfulness of riches, choke the word, and he becometh unfruitful. 23 But he that received seed into the good ground is he that heareth the word, and understandeth it; which also beareth fruit, and bringeth forth, some an hundredfold, some sixty, some thirty.

XIX.

Have you ever ordered your meal, sat there, and ate it, and when you think you've finished up there's a little bit more? That one tater tot or French fry that escaped. It's just sitting there waiting. God is like that in our lives. We think we've got it all figured out, but there's always a little more or rather a lot more, with God. We get a blessing and it's more than we expected. God shows us something new, a new revelation. A deeper understanding about God. We can't even imagine all that God is able to do. Just when you think that's all there is, there's a little more.

Eph 3:20 KJV Now unto him that is able to do exceeding abundantly above all that we ask or think, according to the power that worketh in us.

XX.

Have you ever been around small children that were learning to walk? They may have been your children, or they may have not been. Either way, you get very excited watching them take those steps. If they fall, you don't give up on them. Instead you help them back up. They may not realize is the whole time there is someone there waiting to catch them if they stumble, but there is. We stand ready to keep them from falling or to help them up if they do. I find it comforting that God puts us on the right path and, knowing that we're going to trip up at times, stays with us. He doesn't give up on us when we fall; He just helps us back up. He provides the way to help us not have to stay down when we fall.

Psa 37:23-24 ISV 23 A man's steps are established by the LORD, and the LORD delights in his way. 24 Though he stumbles, he will not fall down flat, for the LORD will hold up his hand.

XXI.

At some point in our lives, we meet someone, and we fall in love with them. We begin to plan a future together, talking about wanting to spend the rest of our lives together. The day finally comes that we get married. We began enjoying the excitement of everyday life. Then days turn into months, and months turn into years. The excitement we felt at the beginning begins to fade away. We go to work, wash clothes, wash dishes, cook supper and live. Things change as we begin to grow older. Oftentimes people begin to look elsewhere for entertainment and adventure. Can I tell you though, this is the adventure. Living our lives together, growing old together (remember being excited about that). We get to go through the seasons of our lives together and love each other. You can see the definition of adventure here: an unusual and exciting, typically hazardous, experience or activity. How well does the definition fit marriage, because it is unusual, it is exciting, and sometimes, yes, it can be hazardous. It is definitely exploring the unknown because none of us know our futures, and to have someone beside you for that future is amazing. So, enjoy your marriage and enjoy time with your spouse and kids. This is the adventure of your lifetime.

1 Corinthians 13: 4-7 NLT

4 Love is patient and kind. Love is not jealous or boastful or proud 5 or rude. It does not demand its own way. It is not irritable, and it keeps no record of being wronged. 6 It does not rejoice about injustice but rejoices whenever the truth wins out. 7 Love never gives up, never loses faith, is always hopeful, and endures through every circumstance.

XXII.

My Uncle Fred was quite the character, he always had something funny to say. He also was a very good welder and didn't mind telling folks that. He often said he could weld anything from the crack of dawn to a broken heart. One guy once made the comment "How good can you weld?" Uncle Fred in his fashion told him "I can weld that tire on your truck to the ground." Now, we know that he couldn't actually weld these things, but it sure was funny. God, on the other hand, can do what He says. He can bind up the broken hearted. He can set you free from anything, and He will forgive you. Just ask Him and believe, for with God anything is possible.

Eph 3:20 KJV Now unto him that is able to do exceeding abundantly above all that we ask or think, according to the power that worketh in us,

Luke 4:18 KJV The Spirit of the Lord is upon me, because he hath anointed me to preach the gospel to the poor; he hath sent me to heal the brokenhearted, to preach deliverance to the captives, and recovering of sight to the blind, to set at liberty them that are bruised, (NET version says: set free those who are oppressed)

XXIII.

A pet peeve of mine is for someone to ignore me, be it in person or in text. If I have taken the time to communicate with someone, I expect a response. Usually if someone ignores me when I'm speaking to them, it's because they are distracted. Most of the time nowadays they are distracted by their phones. When I text someone, it may be that they are busy and don't have time to look at the message. Perhaps they saw the message, but they are so busy they forget to respond. I do understand we live busy lives, and I don't expect people to drop everything to respond to me immediately. At some point though, I expect a response, and it is very bothersome to be ignored.

Isaiah 55:11 So shall my word be that goeth forth out of my mouth: it shall not return unto me void, but it shall accomplish that which I please, and it shall prosper in the thing whereto I sent it.

God sends His Word out to us be it audible by the preached Word of God. He also communicates with us through the written Word of God. We must be careful to let God's Word work in us and respond to it. Because if we don't respond to it, the very Word sent out to be a blessing could turn into a curse. Remember, God said His Word would not return void, it will accomplish something. In Deuteronomy it says it will be a blessing if you obey God's Word and a curse if you don't. The very Word will judge us. So given the choice why not allow the Word to be a blessing as it is intended and respond to it and let it do a good work in us. Don't be too distracted that we miss what God is trying to tell us.

Deuteronomy 11:26-28 KJV 26 Behold, I set before you this day a blessing and a curse; 27 A blessing, if ye obey the commandments of the LORD your God, which I command you this day: 28 And a curse, if ye will not obey the commandments of the LORD your God, but turn aside out of the way which I command you this day, to go after other gods, which ye have not known.

XXIV.

How many times have you been dragging an extension cord, or a water hose and it gets hung up on something? I've even made the comment that if I ever jump out of an airplane, I don't need a parachute just give me an extension cord, it'll hang on something before I hit the ground. You know why, they're loose, or unstable. If you are dragging a board or straight piece of pipe the likelihood of it getting hung up on something is low. You ever see somebody that gets hung up on every little thing. They let so much get them riled up. They are unstable and not totally leaning on God. We have to stand firm in our faith and trust God, really trust God. Live for God, not just casually because that will get you hung up on things. Be a good soldier.

2Ti 2:4 KJV No man that warreth entangleth himself with the affairs of this life; that he may please him who hath chosen him to be a soldier.

XXV.

We have a local car wash that has an attendant out front that will scrub down your car before you enter the car wash. He also will give you instructions. You can hear him loudly say "put it in neutral, hands off the wheel, foot off the brake." Then you enter the car wash. It's loud, it's shaking your car. You have low visibility, there is water and stuff coming from all different directions. It's like a horrible storm. If you were to panic, throw your vehicle in drive and punch the gas or the brake. You would do an incredible amount of damage and possibly hurt yourself. On the other hand, if you just trust the process, you'll come out clean on the other side.

We should trust God's process this way. God may be telling us, put it in neutral, hands off the wheel, foot off the brake. Just go through this process, trusting that God is with us and will keep us. Though things may get intense, and we feel like it's about to come apart. Don't panic. Simply ride it out, and you'll come out clean on the other side.

Mat 14:30-31 WEB 30 But when he saw that the wind was strong, he was afraid, and beginning to sink, he cried out, saying, "Lord, save me!" 31 Immediately Jesus stretched out his hand, took hold of him, and said to him, "You of little faith, why did you doubt?"

Pro 3:5 KJV Trust in the LORD with all thine heart; and lean not unto thine own understanding.

XXVI.

Have you ever gotten hungry for something and just didn't know what you wanted? You end up eating all kinds of stuff trying to fulfill the craving. By the time you're done you're so full yet still haven't satisfied your craving. There are times though that you do know exactly what you want, and you get it. It just hits the spot. You may be out there trying to fill your spiritual appetite with things that won't satisfy you. It may be a job, a relationship or whatever. Often people doing this find themselves bouncing from job to job or relationship to relationship. You find yourself frustrated and full of things that aren't satisfying. You're depressed, aggravated, and still longing for what your soul desires. Stop trying to fill your spiritual appetite with things other than what it really desires. Turn to God, read His Word, and satisfy your soul.

Psa 34:8 KJV O taste and see that the LORD is good: blessed is the man that trusteth in him.

XXVII.

I remember I just felt a great heaviness one day. I was crying and talking to God, and I asked why do you love me so much? At this point my little boy, Joshua, walked up to me to have me pick him up. I felt God impress upon me the answer because you're my child. Think about that. As parents, we love our children dearly. Do you know that God loves us more than we love our children? In Isaiah 49 the Word asks can a woman forget her child and then it says yes, she can. Then it says: But as for me, I'll never forget you! 16 Look! I've inscribed you on the palms of my hands, and your walls are forever before me. So, when you're looking down on yourself and thinking that God doesn't love you. Remember that He does and always will.

1Jn 3:1 KJV Behold, what manner of love the Father hath bestowed upon us, that we should be called the sons of God: therefore the world knoweth us not, because it knew him not.

2Co 6:18 KJV And will be a Father unto you, and ye shall be my sons and daughters, saith the Lord Almighty.

XXVIII.

I had this tree that had mostly been taken down. There was a large stump about 8 feet tall that I needed gone. After a long time, I finally decided to tackle it. I gathered the limbs from around it, piling them up close. Then I began the process of burning it down. I was concerned that this was going to take a long time because of the size of the stump. I got on one side and saw a hollowed-out hole in the center that I had forgotten about. So, I then began to get the center caught on fire. Once it started, it was a quick process. The fire consumed the rottenness from the inside and the stump was burned out in a matter of days. I had to keep restacking loose limbs and such, but it went very well. We too can burn the rottenness out of our lives by letting the fire of the Holy Ghost burn within us. Change has to start from the inside.

Mat 3:11 KJV I indeed baptize you with water unto repentance: but he that cometh after me is mightier than I, whose shoes I am not worthy to bear: he shall baptize you with the Holy Ghost, and with fire.

Mat 23:26 BBE You blind Pharisee, first make clean the inside of the cup and of the plate, so that the outside may become equally clean.

XXIX.

If you know anything about fruit trees, you know there are self-pollinating trees and cross pollinating. The self-pollinating trees do not need other trees present to produce fruit. Whereas cross pollinating trees do need other trees in order to produce fruit. We are not self-pollinating trees; we have to be in Jesus to produce fruit as well as in the body of Christ. We need the church, and the church needs us. We need each other to cross pollinate. We help each other develop and produce fruit in the kingdom of God.

Joh 15:5 KJV I am the vine, ye are the branches: He that abideth in me, and I in him, the same bringeth forth much fruit: for without me ye can do nothing.

Mat 7:20 KJV Wherefore by their fruits ye shall know them.

Gal 5:22-23 ISV 22 But the fruit of the Spirit is love, joy, peace, patience, kindness, goodness, faithfulness, 23 gentleness, and self-control. There is no law against such things.

XXX.

I remember my Uncle Fred telling me about a man that had done him wrong. He was furious about it. He told my Uncle Dave, his brother, who told him to just be nice to the man. Uncle Fred thought this sounded crazy, but he took Uncle Dave's advice anyway. After some time, the man approached Uncle Fred and told him that he was driving him crazy, being nice. He told Uncle Fred that he knew he'd done wrong and apologized. Uncle Dave understood having peace in the situation. He understood Biblical concepts. I remember a similar situation with a friend at work. He told me that our supervisor just didn't like him. I suggested that he pray for the supervisor. A couple months later I was sitting in the breakroom and another coworker was complaining about someone that was giving them trouble. My friend piped up, "Pray for them." Apparently, he had heeded my advice and it worked so well that he was now telling others to do the same. So, if you are dealing with a similar situation, try taking the high road. Pray and be at peace.

Rom 12:20 Easy English But you should do this: 'If your enemy is hungry, feed him. If he needs to drink, give him something to drink. If you do these things, your enemy will become ashamed. He will become sorry because of what he did to you.'

Mat 5:44 WEB But I tell you, love your enemies, bless those who curse you, do good to those who hate you, and pray for those who mistreat you and persecute you,

XXXI.

Have you ever gone to great lengths to give someone a gift? You plan it out, you find the perfect gift, you spend your hard-earned money. It was okay though because you were excited about giving them this gift. Then you finally give it to them and it's almost like you gave them a box of rocks. You've now lost all your excitement and are angry. You may give them another gift at some point, but you may be less apt to go to great lengths to give them another gift of the same value or thought. I wonder if God gets this way with us, when He gives us great blessings, and we don't return to give thanks. In the story of the lepers in Luke 17:11-19, Jesus performed a miracle, and the lepers were cleansed. Only one returned to give thanks, and he was made whole. How many miracles do we deny ourselves because we don't give thanks? Giving thanks is mentioned over 170 times in the Bible, so it is very important to God.

1Ch 29:13 KJV Now therefore, our God, we thank thee, and praise thy glorious name.

XXXII.

Have you ever come across a tree that had something grown into it that shouldn't have been there? I've seen fencing, decorations and even electrical wiring grown into trees. The problem is the two things were too close in proximity, and while the tree grew, the foreign object became part of it. I have also seen though, trees that refused to let something become part of them that shouldn't be. My daddy had thrown a rubber boot into the fork of a tree trying to get something out of the tree before I was born. I just grew up seeing it way up there. In the process of time the tree died. I remember walking up and seeing the small piece of boot laying to the side. The tree, even till death, refused to let what didn't belong to become part of it. In life we are going to come in contact with things that don't need to be a part of who we are. We can either be like the trees that allow things to become part of them that don't need to be there. Or we can refuse to let it become part of who we are.

1 Corinthians 7:31

NLT

31 Those who use the things of the world should not become attached to them. For this world as we know it will soon pass away.

2Co 6:17 KJV Wherefore come out from among them, and be ye separate, saith the Lord, and touch not the unclean thing; and I will receive you,

XXXIII.

Electrical conduit is a tube used to protect and route electrical wiring in a building or structure. Electrical conduit may be made of metal, plastic, fiber, or fired clay. Most conduit is rigid, but flexible conduit is used for some purposes. In the production of conduit, it goes from a flat form into a bending and shaping process. While in this process, it is heated to make it more pliable, but water is added to make sure it doesn't break or damage during the process. We should be like conduit. We should protect the power and help route it or direct it into a building (other people). We all may be made up of different materials because we all have different backgrounds, experiences, and personalities. Some of us may be rigid, some may be flexible, but our job is the same. Protect and deliver the power. You may ask yourself; how do I protect the power? One way is to protect God's image by being Christ-like and not carnal. In other words, be a good person. The other is to stay in His Word and in prayer so that the power can work within you.

We have to allow God to bend and shape us into what He intends us to be. It may get hot in the trials. It may get uncomfortable, but the Holy Ghost (water) will be there to make sure we aren't damaged or broken beyond use.

1Co 3:9 KJV For we are labourers together with God: ye are God's husbandry, ye are God's building.

XXXIV.

My little boy, Isaac, recently had to have antibiotic ear drops put in his ear. The instructions said he had to stay on his side for 2 minutes. This was not a fun process, but he needed it to get better. Why 2 minutes you may ask. So, the drops can soak all the way into the deepest part of the ear. I wonder how many times God tries to drop something in our spirit, but we don't sit and let it soak in. We hop up and on our way. We need to linger and let God make us better.

Jas 1:22-25 ISV 22 Keep on being obedient to the word, and not merely being hearers who deceive themselves. 23 For if anyone hears the word but is not obedient to it, he is like a man who looks at himself in a mirror 24 and studies himself carefully, and then goes off and immediately forgets what he looks like. 25 But the one who looks at the perfect law of freedom and remains committed to it—thereby demonstrating that he is not a forgetful hearer but a doer of what that law requires—will be blessed in what he does.

1 Peter 2:12

NLT

12 Be careful to live properly among your unbelieving neighbors. Then even if they accuse you of doing wrong, they will see your honorable behavior, and they will give honor to God when he judges the world.

XXXV.

We see people dressed in ways and talking in ways that often cause our demeanor to change a little. We think they should know better, but that's the thing. They don't. They've been raised that way, and it's their normal. You see, cannibals that are raised in that lifestyle probably don't see anything wrong with eating humans. I mean it's their normal. It disgusts us, or does it? In Galatians 5:15 KJV But if ye bite and devour one another, take heed that ye be not consumed one of another.

We may not actually eat other people physically, but we may eat them up with our words and actions. Many of us grew up this way so we don't see anything wrong with it. It's "our" normal. How do we avoid this? Walk in the Spirit and not the lust of the flesh. Crucify the flesh. Develop the fruit of the Spirit and live in the Spirit.

Gal 5:14-16 KJV 14 For all the law is fulfilled in one word, even in this; Thou shalt love thy neighbour as thyself. 15 But if ye bite and devour one another, take heed that ye be not consumed one of another. 16 This I say then, Walk in the Spirit, and ye shall not fulfil the lust of the flesh.

Gal 5:22-25 KJV 22 But the fruit of the Spirit is love, joy, peace, longsuffering, gentleness, goodness, faith, 23 Meekness, temperance: against such there is no law. 24 And they that are Christ's have crucified the flesh with the affections and lusts. 25 If we live in the Spirit, let us also walk in the Spirit.

XXXVI.

I was at the zoo with my family one day. There were times we were mere feet away from animals that in their natural habitat are forces to be reckoned with and majestic to say the least. Yet, here they are, tigers, elephants, leopards, eagles, lions, and many others, just laying around waiting for someone to feed them. Totally dependent upon the zookeepers to provide what they need. It got me thinking, how did these animals wind up here? After a little research I found a few ways, animals end up in zoos. 1. They are captured from the wild. From their natural habitat. 2. The animal was injured and never healed correctly. 3. Some are simply born into zoo's 4. Some come from other zoos. Often from animals that have been born at these other zoos. Now I don't want to ruin zoos for you but follow me for a moment. These animals are in captivity. Just like these animals, some of us are also in captivity. We should be forces to be reckoned with, but we are caged. We should be operating in the kingdom of God, which is our natural habitat once we've been born again. Yet we sit quietly, and wait to be fed. Yes, we may raise a ruckus every now and again, but we never break free. Some of us were captured by something that stole away our fire. Some of us were injured and never healed correctly. Some of us are born into captivity because our parents never broke free. Then some are captive and move from church to church staying in captivity and never breaking free. We don't have to stay in captivity. We can break free and stay free. Jesus paid the price for us to live free. Break free and live for God fervently

    2Ti 2:26 KJV And that they may recover themselves out of the snare of the devil, who are taken captive by him at his will.

1Co 6:19-20 KJV 19 What? know ye not that your body is the temple of the Holy Ghost which is in you, which ye have of God, and ye are not your own? 20 For ye are bought with a price: therefore glorify God in your body, and in your spirit, which are God's.

XXXVII.

Have you ever been walking through your house at night and hit your toe on something? Your entire body knows it immediately. You stop what you are doing and take a second to recover and get your composure. You may even need to repent if you found out there was something in your heart that you didn't know was there. With this in mind, we are the body of Christ. We should always be attentive to the body and make sure each other member is okay. I want to give you a different perspective, though. If you look up the body parts and their functions, you can quickly see how they compare to the body of Christ. The body needs all of its parts to do what they are supposed to do in order to function correctly. Somebody has to be that toe that is more sensitive to things and may detect things that the rest of the body may miss. Somebody has to be the kidneys that filter out the stuff that's bad for the body. The eyes, the ears, and the mouth we always think about, but what about the knuckles that get skinned up doing the work. Then someone has to be the rear end that discharges the useless things in the body (you know you laughed; you were probably already thinking it.) The point is you may not be the mouth, you may be the knuckles, but without you the body wouldn't be complete. Embrace your role and function completely in it.

Rom 12:4-5 KJV 4 For as we have many members in one body, and all members have not the same office: 5 So we, being many, are one body in Christ, and every one members one of another.

XXXVIII.

We see them everywhere, decorative crosses. Hanging on walls, sitting on tabletops, even hanging around people's necks. I mean, they are nice decorations, right. They have all these designs in them and are supposed to tell people "Hey I'm a Christian." Unfortunately, people misunderstand the Cross; it comes with sacrifice. The Cross of Christ was not pretty. It was bloody, and it was hard. Yet this is how we like Jesus to be in our lives, as a decoration. Something to pretty up our lives, but no sacrifice involved. Let's aim to be more like Jesus and have Him at the center of our lives, not just a decorative ornament.

Gal 2:20 KJV I am crucified with Christ: nevertheless I live; yet not I, but Christ liveth in me: and the life which I now live in the flesh I live by the faith of the Son of God, who loved me, and gave himself for me.

XXXIX.

Have you ever seen someone get a gift, and it was not what they were expecting and not in a good way? Most of us may handle this fine, but some folks lose their minds. This can cause a rift in relationships for years. Often, we act this way with God. We expect God to do things the way we have imagined him to do them.

In 2 Kings 5:11, Naaman had an expectation of not just being healed but how it should have been done. He was disappointed and angry because it didn't happen like he thought it should. Thankfully, someone convinced him to listen, and he received his miracle. He almost missed it because of his expectations of how it should have been.

In Matthew 19:16-22 the rich young ruler had an expectation of how Jesus would respond to his accomplishments. When Jesus didn't respond the way he had expected, he went away sorrowful.

We too will end up angry and sorrowful if we try to live for God expecting Him to do things the way we think they should happen. We can't go pray to God with a multiple choice of how He should handle whatever it is we need. We can pray for whatever we need and leave it in His hands as to how He will handle it. Like the 3 Hebrew boys said God is able to deliver us from the furnace, but if He doesn't, we are still not going to bow. Because He will deliver us out of your hands. They left the "how" up to God. Trust God, not with conditions, but absolutely. He's got this, leave the how up to Him.

Jer 29:11 KJV For I know the thoughts that I think toward you, saith the LORD, thoughts of peace, and not of evil, to give you an expected end.

Isa 55:8-9 KJV 8 For my thoughts are not your thoughts, neither are your ways my ways, saith the LORD. 9 For as the heavens are higher than the earth, so are my ways higher than your ways, and my thoughts than your thoughts.

XL.

I just want some peace! How many times have we heard this or said it ourselves? You ever see somebody whose world looks like it's falling apart, and they just seem at peace. They've most likely found peace in Jesus.

Isa 53:5 KJV But he was wounded for our transgressions, he was bruised for our iniquities: the chastisement of our peace was upon him; and with his stripes we are healed.

I've heard this scripture, read it, and even quoted it. For some reason I overlooked part of it every time. The chastisement of our peace was upon Him. Chastisement is defined as severe criticism; a rebuke or strong reprimand, corporal punishment; a beating. When Jesus was being taunted, rebuked, criticized and just all around chastised by the soldiers and those around. He took that for our peace. Can you imagine going through the beating, the crown of thorns, carrying the cross. All while being yelled at from all around. That would be enough to drive anyone crazy. Jesus took all of that so when the world and everything around us is going crazy, we can have peace.

Joh 14:27 BBE May peace be with you; my peace I give to you: I give it not as the world gives. Let not your heart be troubled; let it be without fear.

XLI.

Many of us have heard this story, but it bears repeating. There was a man walking one foggy night when he accidentally stepped off the side of a cliff. Grasping in the darkness he caught a small tree growing out of the side of the cliff. He began to cry out for help. After some time of calling, he hears a voice say, "This is God, " to which the man cries "Oh, God, help me! " Then God responds, "Do you believe in Me?" The man in desperation says "Yes, Lord, I believe. " To which God replies, "Let go of the tree." After a quiet pause, the man says "Is there anybody else up there? " We laugh at this but how often is this us? Trust God. We put it on plaques and hang it up. We read it and say that's right. Yet we do the opposite. We trust man more than God every day. We trust that the guy coming down the road isn't going to lose control and swerve into us. We trust the man-made vehicles we drive to run correctly and protect us in the event of an accident. We trust the doctors' reports more than the scriptures that we have on healing. You see we say "Trust God," and then question if we really can. Remember this, it's easy to trust when everything is going good. It's when things aren't going well that we really learn to trust. Let us truly trust God, for He can be trusted.

Pro 3:5 KJV Trust in the LORD with all thine heart; and lean not unto thine own understanding.

Psa 118:8 KJV It is better to trust in the LORD than to put confidence in man.

XLII.

So, I have my new house sitting there with no electricity and my old house with electricity. The air conditioner went out in the old house and I'm cooling it with window units. The new house is cooler during the heat of the day than the old house, even though it doesn't have electricity or power. So, the difference is insulation. The new house has way better insulation than the old house. This got me to thinking that we need to be insulated from the world, and our insulation is holiness and separation. That's why sometimes you see people that don't have Jesus or the power, but they are calm, cool, and collective inside because they have separated themselves from the world. This is also why you see people with Jesus (power) that are coming apart. They haven't insulated or separated themselves from the world. Let us make sure that we are "insulated" from the outside world.

2Co 6:17 KJV Wherefore come out from among them, and be ye separate, saith the Lord, and touch not the unclean thing; and I will receive you,

XLIII.

My daddy was quite a prankster throughout his life. He once grabbed a chicken snake by the tail, popped it like a whip, and broke its neck. He then takes the dead snake swings it around over his head like a lasso. At this point, his unsuspecting brother, my Uncle Fred, hears "Fred!" When he turns around my dad releases the snake hurling it at my uncle, with the intentions of it going over his head and scaring him. That is not what happened. The dead snake hit my uncle in the neck wrapping around his neck completely. I can only imagine him frantically removing the snake and trying to get free of it. After some "intense fellowship" between them, all was good. Because honestly, they were both pranksters, and my Uncle Fred could give as good as he could get. Aren't we often like Uncle Fred? Something finds its way into our lives that appears to be a threat. Then we lose all composure and frantically respond to the situation around us. What we should do is reach out to God in prayer. Let us trust God the way Paul did and shook off the snake in the fire.

Pro 3:5 KJV Trust in the LORD with all thine heart; and lean not unto thine own understanding.

XLIV.

I was sitting on my porch one morning just looking around and I looked up and saw the clouds moving. It just hit me, even though I can't feel the winds moving, and even though I don't feel it the earth is moving. According to science the Earth spins at about a 1000 miles per hour, the winds at cloud height can be undetermined speeds. Even though we don't feel the movement, there's always movement. Likewise, just because we don't see God working doesn't mean he isn't. Quite honestly the stillness here on Earth keeps us calm. So, know that God is always working and moving, trust Him in the stillness.

Psa 46:10 KJV Be still, and know that I am God: I will be exalted among the heathen, I will be exalted in the earth.

XLV. A Sheep in Wolf's Clothing

That's right, a sheep in wolf's clothing, not a typo. So, what am I talking about? You see we are the sheep of His pasture. Jesus says in Matthew 10 that He sends us forth as sheep in the midst of wolves. It's inevitable that we be around people that don't have God as their main priority. They are more focused on self, they are worldly.

Phi 3:19 ISV Their destiny is destruction, their god is their belly, and their glory is in their shame. Their minds are set on worldly things.

If all your friends are worldly, and instead of you influencing them they are influencing you, then there lies the problem. If you, who are supposed to be a sheep, are hanging out with wolves. If you are dressing like them, acting like them, talking like them, then you are becoming a sheep in wolf's clothing. This will destroy you, just as a sheep would be destroyed by wolves. Now you may say, well Jesus said I send you forth as sheep among wolves and you'd be right. He also said in the same verse to be wise as serpents and gentle as doves. Meaning be attentive, be different and be kind. Four animals were mentioned in one verse and never once did it say blend in and be like them. You are not meant to be like them. You are meant to be different.

2Co 6:17 KJV Wherefore come out from among them, and be ye separate, saith the Lord, and touch not the unclean thing; and I will receive you,

Romans 12:2 NLT

2 Don't copy the behavior and customs of this world, but let God transform you into a new person by changing the way you think. Then you will learn to know God's will for you, which is good and pleasing and perfect.

The thing is we have to be in the world but not of the world. We have to change those around us, not the other way around. We have to reach others but not fall out of the boat in the process.

Jud 1:23 ISV Save others by snatching them from the fire. To others, show mercy with fear, hating even the clothes stained by their sinful lives.

Proverbs 12:26 The righteous choose their friends carefully, but the way of the wicked leads them astray.

Proverbs 27:17 As iron sharpens iron, so a friend sharpens a friend.

Proverbs 13:20 Walk with the wise and become wise; associate with fools and get in trouble.

So let me be clear. You can and will have friends that are "in the world." Choose your friends wisely though. The thing is, make sure that they are not pulling you away from God. If anyone is pulling you away from God, they are not your friend. You should be helping your worldly friends get closer to Jesus. How much better if you and your friends are helping each other get closer to Christ?

XLVI.

I came across some fake diamonds, and it got me to thinking. Obviously, they are fake. If one didn't know, however, at first glance they may look genuine. Upon a closer look, though, you'd be able to tell. If they didn't convince you, you could then put them to the test. They'd crack or even be demolished under pressure. Turn up the heat and they wouldn't be able to take it. Why? Because they aren't real, they haven't been crushed under extreme pressure to be made into what they were. They didn't have to go through all the things it takes to make a real diamond. Hence, they can't endure and don't have the same value. When it feels like you are being put under a lot of pressure. Just remember that God is making you into something more valuable.

Isa 43:4 BBE Because of your value in my eyes, you have been honoured, and loved by me....

XLVII.

I had to cut a couple of trees down recently, and I had removed them to another place on my property to burn. A couple of weeks later, as I was walking around the place where they were, I noticed that I had never removed the small limbs that had broken off. You couldn't see them from a distance, but they were there. Once I gathered them, I had filled my little lawnmower trailer to the brim with them. We sometimes cut something out of our lives so we can improve our life. Afterwards, we may just move on thinking well that's done. Then one day we see something sticking out that we thought was completely gone. Often when we cut something out of our lives, fragments may fall in random places. So, then we have to clean the rest of it out of our lives. So don't get discouraged when you see remnants that you have cut out of your life. It doesn't mean that you never conquered it. It may just be fallen fragments.

Eph 4:22-24 WEB 22 that you put away, as concerning your former way of life, the old man that grows corrupt after the lusts of deceit, 23 and that you be renewed in the spirit of your mind, 24 and put on the new man, who in the likeness of God has been created in righteousness and holiness of truth.

XLVIII.

You hear it every summer, man I can't wait for it to get cool. Then in the winter, man I can't wait for it to get warm. When the season gets uncomfortable, we want it to change. You know what we can do to make the seasons change? Nothing. We just have to wait. You may be going through a season in your life that is uncomfortable, and you just want it to change. Just keep holding on and trusting God. Because the seasons change, you just have to wait and be patient.

Psa 27:14 KJV Wait on the LORD: be of good courage, and he shall strengthen thine heart: wait, I say, on the LORD.

Ecc 3:1 KJV To every thing there is a season, and a time to every purpose under the heaven:

XLIX.

Have you ever observed the chaos in a home right after Christmas? Toys, boxes, wrapping paper, etc. just spread out everywhere. You look over your home and don't know where to start. You find a place to start and get everything picked up straightened back up. Then you can breathe. If you find yourself feeling like this, like everything is out of place in your life. If you are depressed, stressed, or just feel lost in all the craziness. You may be thinking that you don't know where to start. I can tell you to start with Jesus. Know that Jesus can bring you peace and put all the pieces back together. Reach out to Him.

Phi 4:7 KJV And the peace of God, which passeth all understanding, shall keep your hearts and minds through Christ Jesus.

L.

My nephew and I were in this store many years ago, and we came across this Christmas tree for sale. I commented about it being a pink tree, to which he responded it's not pink it's white. I told him no it's pink, again he said it's white. This went back and forth for a few minutes until I asked a cashier at the store, and she said it's white sir. I responded to her with nope you're wrong too, it's pink. Of course, I was being facetious. Now, what the problem was that it was a white tree with red lights on it, and I'm slightly color blind. So, to me the tree was pink, that is the way I saw it, and nobody was going to convince me otherwise. You would think I would have taken my nephew's word about the tree right off because I knew that I have trouble with some colors. I can see colors, but just have a problem differentiating between some. The point is when someone tries to share the gospel of Jesus Christ with you, don't be like I was with the tree. Just because you don't see it that way doesn't mean that the person you are talking to is wrong. It may just mean that you have a "blindness" to it. You may be familiar with the word of God and know a lot, but it could be that you just can't see it clearly. Your vision may be blurred. Please be open to help. Check what they say against the scripture. Pray that your eyes may be open to the scripture that you may see clearly.

Psa 119:18 BBE Let my eyes be open to see the wonders of your law.

If you are the person sharing the gospel, please be patient. Because the person you're sharing with may not have the ability to see what you see. You may have to help them open their eyes.

LI.

I wanted to share a little perspective with you. Perhaps your Christmas didn't go like you wanted. Maybe you didn't get that gift that you wanted or didn't get as many as you wanted. Maybe the people you were expecting to come over didn't. Maybe you burnt the Christmas meal. Now you're upset because that just ruined your Christmas. Well, I was told a story by a friend that had been in Walmart just before Christmas and saw the police talking to a lady who had tried to shoplift something. When he inquired, he learned that the lady was homeless and wanted to be arrested because she would at least have something to eat and a warm place to sleep. So, if you're upset over Christmas happenings, maybe you should count your blessings and not your gifts. Or just look at the good and not the bad. Be thankful for what you do have.

1Th 5:18 KJV In every thing give thanks: for this is the will of God in Christ Jesus concerning you.

LII.

I was asked once what I felt love was. So, here is my opinion. Love is working crazy hours to supply for your family. Love is sleeping on a floor to be close to your kids because they are sick. Love is doing without the things you want, and often need, to supply for your loved ones. Love is dealing with inconveniences. Love is working a full day and having to spend the night awake deprived of sleep because your loved one has to go to the hospital, all while keeping their spirits up. Love is bringing someone a cup of coffee. Love is laughing and crying with each other. Love is holding on during hard times. Love is sometimes letting go. Love is giving in sometimes, but love is also standing your ground when it's needed. Love is ignoring the pain in your body to take care of your loved ones. Love is tough, stern talks, times of listening and lots of joking. Love is walking through your house in the middle of the night covering people up. Love is praying for your family. Love is a pat on the back, a home cooked meal, a point in the right direction. Love is encouragement when you're down and a call to reality when you're doing wrong. Love is not always fun and sometimes even painful, but it is always worth it. Most of all love is our Savior going to a cross even though He knew some would never turn to him. Love is forgiveness of our sins and paying a debt that we could never pay. Love is...

1 Cor 13: 4-7 NLT

4 Love is patient and kind. Love is not jealous or boastful or proud 5 or rude. It does not demand its own way. It is not irritable, and it keeps no record of being wronged. 6 It does not rejoice about injustice but rejoices whenever the truth wins out. 7 Love never gives up, never loses faith, is always hopeful, and endures through every circumstance.

LIII.

What would you think of a lifeguard that didn't know how to swim? Or if he showed up and didn't pay attention to his surroundings? What if he didn't care about people? Ridiculous as you may think this sounds, we as Christians are lifeguards. We are supposed to help save people from drowning in sin. Yet we don't train in the Word of God to prepare ourselves. We get so caught up in our little world that we stop paying attention to those around us. God forbid that we get to the point that we don't like people. We have to strive to do our best. We have to love people and reach for them. Because we are lifeguards.

2Ti 2:15 KJV Study to shew thyself approved unto God, a workman that needeth not to be ashamed, rightly dividing the word of truth.

Jud 1:23 KJV And others save with fear, pulling them out of the fire; hating even the garment spotted by the flesh.

LIV.

We all have something that we may have a take it or leave it attitude towards. It may be a type of food, drink or even activity. The truth is that is not a problem because we all have our likes and dislikes. The problem arises when we have a take it or leave it attitude towards Jesus. We live carelessly in life with little to no thought of Jesus through our day. We can talk about the weather, the news, work, etc., yet unfortunately, we don't spend much of our time talking about our Creator and Savior. We have things that we absolutely have to do. We have to have our coffee, watch our TV show, do this or that, whatever it may be. But spending time with Jesus is a take it or leave it thing. We should strive to make Jesus the center of our lives. So today, spend some time talking to Jesus, read some Bible, go to church, and participate. Remember Jesus loved us enough to give His life for us, we should love Him enough to live for Him.

Jos 24:15 KJV And if it seem evil unto you to serve the LORD, choose you this day whom ye will serve; whether the gods which your fathers served that were on the other side of the flood, or the gods of the Amorites, in whose land ye dwell: but as for me and my house, we will serve the LORD.

LV.

I heard a story about a woman that was in a testimony service. People were telling everyone about how God had blessed them. She, at some point, said that she envied those whom God had provided for in their desperate need. She admitted that she had never been in those situations because she always had plenty of money. It got me thinking about grace. Grace is not amazing, until you receive forgiveness of your sins. Grace is not amazing, until you have failed over and over and still Jesus picks you back up. Grace is not amazing until you are surrounded by your accusers and walk away free. Grace is not amazing until you are at the end of your rope, and you are lifted by His precious love. Grace is not amazing until you share it. Grace is not amazing until you find yourself in need of it. When you find yourself in need of it don't underestimate grace, because it's always available and it is amazing.

Rom 5:20-21 KJV 20 Moreover the law entered, that the offence might abound. But where sin abounded, grace did much more abound: 21 That as sin hath reigned unto death, even so might grace reign through righteousness unto eternal life by Jesus Christ our Lord.

2Co 13:14 KJV The grace of the Lord Jesus Christ, and the love of God, and the communion of the Holy Ghost, be with you all. Amen.

LVI.

I had this fig tree in my yard that I noticed had figs on it, but the rest of the tree looked dead. As a matter of fact, everything around it looked dead. Most of us know the story of Jesus cursing the fig tree. For those that might not here you go.

Matthew 21:19 KJV And when he saw a fig tree in the way, he came to it, and found nothing thereon, but leaves only, and said unto it, let no fruit grow on thee henceforward forever. And presently the fig tree withered away...

So here Jesus curses the fig tree because it was not producing fruit. The thought I wanted to share is this. Be like this fig tree in the picture. When everything is dead around you, and it seems like everything is against you, when everyone would understand why you aren't producing fruit. When life has you down, press on. Produce fruit anyway, go against the odds and bring forth fruit.

2Ti 4:2 WEB preach the word; be urgent in season and out of season; reprove, rebuke, and exhort with all patience and teaching.

Galatians 5:22 NET But the fruit of the Spirit is love, joy, peace, patience, kindness, goodness, faithfulness, 23 gentleness, and self-control. Against such things there is no law.

LVII.

I saw an old dead tree the other day in the middle of a patch of lively pine trees. It stuck out like a sore thumb. It was taller than the pines and drew your attention. Then it came to me. You may have something in your life that once was alive and well, but now is dead. You just want it gone, but it just stands there. It's an eye sore in your life, it's rottenness disgusts you. There is life all around it, but you focus on the deadness that you see. Just hold on because that which is dead can grow no longer. Just as all the pine trees will outgrow the dead tree and you'll no longer see it. The good things in your life will outgrow the dead things. Eventually the dead stuff will crumble and fall, fertilizing the things in your life that need to grow.

Rom 8:18 BBE I am of the opinion that there is no comparison between the pain of this present time and the glory which we will see in the future.

1Pe 1:6-7 NET 6 This brings you great joy, although you may have to suffer for a short time in various trials. 7 Such trials show the proven character of your faith, which is much more valuable than gold – gold that is tested by fire, even though it is passing away – and will bring praise and glory and honor when Jesus Christ is revealed.

LVIII.

I have had a few conversations over time with folks that question their value to the kingdom of God. They think that they aren't having any effect. I've heard stuff like, "Well, I don't really hear from God like other people do," or, "I don't really have a ministry like others." So, I wanted to share some of the things that we shared. Many people forget about Ananias in the Bible that prayed for Paul and helped convert him. That's all that is ever said about Ananias, but he is connected to everything that Paul ever did. From every soul Paul helped to the epistles that he wrote, Ananias had a tie to. If Paul was the only person that Ananias ever helped, what a ministry he had. Then consider Paul wrote in 1 Corinthians 12 about the body of Christ. Consider your own body, which part is unimportant to you, and you are willing to part with? Just because you may not do what another part of the body does, does not mean that you are unimportant? On the contrary, think of the fact of how difficult it is for a body to perform without what may seem like an insignificant part. Losing any part of the body affects the entire body. Even a small paper cut changes our body's entire focus to help the part of the body that is injured. Paul goes on to write in the same chapter about ministries (It is no coincidence that this all ends up in the same chapter). This is where he speaks of the apostles, prophets, and teachers. He also speaks of gifts of healing and miracles. But in the same scripture he mentions the gift of helps. Just being a help to your brother or sister is a ministry. It may be an encouraging word, a helping hand or even a smile. Never underestimate your ministry or significance because without one part of the body how would the rest be affected.

Mar 9:41 KJV For whosoever shall give you a cup of water to drink in my name, because ye belong to Christ, verily I say unto you, he shall not lose his reward.

LIX.

What if God wanted you to be a good parent? So, you know if you are a parent, then you are called to be a good, godly parent. Someone had to raise the heroes of Faith, be they in the Bible or just people we know. Yes, I know they all had to have an encounter with God to get them where they were, but there had been someone in their life to help them get there. What if you were called to raise a man or woman of God? Would they make it? Would they love God? Would they know how to pray? What attributes would they have, good or bad? Now don't lose hope. If you have not done the best at this, then get up and start now. As it says in Ephesians: bring them up by training and instructing them about the Lord. In Deuteronomy it should be part of who we are, it should just pour out of us, and it will if that's what we are full of. I find it interesting right after the commandment is given: love the LORD thy God with all thine heart, and with all thy soul, and with all thy might. That the first thing that comes up is live it and live it in front of your children. So, believe it or not, if you are a parent then this is part of your calling. So, make your calling and election sure and let's do our best to point our children towards heaven.

Deu 6:5-7 KJV 5 And thou shalt love the LORD thy God with all thine heart, and with all thy soul, and with all thy might. 6 And these words, which I command thee this day, shall be in thine heart: 7 And thou shalt teach them diligently unto thy children, and shalt talk of them when thou sittest in thine house, and when thou walkest by the way, and when thou liest down, and when thou risest up.

Now I know there are some parents that have been diligent about this and their children may not be living for God. This is heartbreaking and I hope and pray that one day they will turn to God. For you, remember Jesus' brothers didn't follow Him at first either.

LX.

Around Halloween one year, everyone was talking about horror movies that they were going to watch. It prompted me to consider this. This is a story told from a soldier's point of view, of an incident he was involved in, ages ago. "My name does not matter, but the events I tell you of, do. I was a soldier, and a good one at the time that this harrowing event occurred. It was at night. There was a cold dampness in the air. I was at my post when my commander told me to go assist with an arrest. This was common so I thought nothing of it. We gathered our torches and weapons and proceeded to the place where we were told the criminal would be. As we arrived the criminal had what appeared to be a gang with him. We prepared for their resistance. Only one of them resisted but ceased after their leader told him not to. After we had the prisoner in custody, things began to seem a little weird and even a little suspicious. The first thing we did was carry the prisoner to one trial after the other. This was odd to me because trials were not usually held at night. The evidence that was presented all had holes in it. It did not take me long to figure out that these were mock trials, but I was a good soldier and did as I was told. Finally, as the night turned into day, we brought the prisoner to the high court. I knew it would end this charade that I had been privy to. Unfortunately, it did not. The prisoner was passed from one leader to another as if nobody wanted to handle this case. Finally, we returned to the high court where the official in charge presented the accusers with a proposition. He would release one prisoner to them. This man who they accused or a vile man who I personally had assisted in arresting. Now I thought this would finish this foolishness. Imagine my surprise when they chose the true criminal to be released. From there the original prisoner was sentenced to die. TO DIE!!! I did not understand, but I was a good soldier. We led the prisoner away where he was beaten and mocked by the other soldiers. I have never seen a man beaten to such a degree. One could scarcely tell that he was a man by the time they were through, he looked like a monster from your worst nightmares. My heart had begun to beat harder; my thoughts were spiraling through my head like a violent storm. We then took the prisoner away to be crucified. As he weakly carried his cross up the hill, I could barely stand it. I grabbed an onlooker from the crowd and ordered him to carry this poor man's cross. When we reached the top of the hill, he was nailed to a cross. He hung there for hours, before he finally died. There was an earthquake at that point, and others told me of many things that happened, but they did not matter to me. For I was haunted by the fact that I chose to be a good soldier rather than a good human being and help this man. Days later rumors began to flow around about the man. Some said he was alive from the dead, while others said that his gang stole his body. I do not know which. I now live a life trying my best not to be around people. I am no longer a soldier; I could not do that anymore. I cannot forgive myself, nor do I expect someone else to forgive me. I can barely sleep at night anymore because the images I saw haunt me. I lay awake and wonder if one of his gangs will find me and kill me for being involved. I just wish I would have never been there that night. Or that I would have helped this man they called Jesus.

The horror of this story is not what Jesus went through, though that was terribly horrific. No, it is that there are people just like this soldier who have Jesus come through their lives and they never realize that he is there to help them. He is there to save them. They think they have done too much wrong to be forgiven. Please today stop living in the horror of your past. Seek out Jesus and be set free.

1Ti 1:13-15 KJV 13 Who was before a blasphemer, and a persecutor, and injurious: but I obtained mercy, because I did it ignorantly in unbelief. 14 And the grace of our Lord was exceeding abundant with faith and love which is in Christ Jesus. 15 This is a faithful saying, and worthy of all acceptation, that Christ Jesus came into the world to save sinners; of whom I am chief.

LXI.

I have known many people that have gone on a diet and have succeeded greatly. My oldest daughter Kathryn was one of them. She set her mind to it and did it. It all starts with the decision to lose weight. So, we figure out our plan and then do it for about a week. After that we fall off and eat worse than we did before. We eat more junk food and intake more calories. Then we realize oh no we're gaining weight. And if we continue on this path it could lead to many health problems later in life.

The thing about a diet is what you take in matters. You cannot just eat anything you want and lose weight or expect it not to affect you. You have to watch what you eat. Whether you use keto, calorie counting, or whatever you have to watch what you take in. The same goes for living for God. We can't just take in anything we want and expect to be spiritually healthy. If we take in worldly things, then they will add unwanted weight to us. We fill up on junk and take no time to exercise our faith. We don't pray, we don't read our Bibles, we don't go to church. Then we expect that it will have no effect on us. Just like the physical body, the spiritual body needs attention too. So, decide today that you will change and take in healthy spiritual food for your soul. Shed that unwanted baggage and weight that will only hinder your life.

Hebrews 12:1 KJV Wherefore seeing we also are compassed about with so great a cloud of witnesses, let us lay aside every weight, and the sin which doth so easily beset us, and let us run with patience the race that is set before us,

1 Timothy 4:8 KJV For bodily exercise profiteth little: but godliness is profitable unto all things, having promise of the life that now is, and of that which is to come.

LXII.

I can see you praying now. Sitting in with the lights dimmed, tears running down your face. Asking God, where did I go wrong? Why won't my children live for you? I tried so hard to raise them right. I brought them to church, I led them the right way. Yet they still insist on going their own way. Have you ever read the discourse in John 7 with Jesus and his brothers? Look at verse 5 with me. John 7:5 ISV Not even his brothers believed in him. Read that again, Jesus's brothers didn't believe in Him. That is mind blowing to me. I mean you have the greatest example, the actual way, truth and life, God incarnate himself. Yet you still don't believe! Later on, they would come to believe in Him. His brothers James and Jude would go on to write two books of the Bible. History teaches that they both go on to be martyrs. So, with all that being said, you need to hear this loud and clear. You did good! Take that in for a second and breathe. You try to do the best you can and leave the rest to God. Pray for them and love them but quit beating yourself up.

Pro 22:6 KJV Train up a child in the way he should go: and when he is old, he will not depart from it.

LXIII.

People often admire the beauty of the lighthouses. They appreciate the light that gives them direction and keeps them from harm. This though is not a story about lighthouses. This is the story of a lighthouse keeper. This keeper that we are speaking of was growing tired of his duties, responsibilities, and position. You see, no one ever took time to thank the keeper. Most did not even know the keeper's name. Being a lighthouse keeper was not an exciting job. Sometimes it was lonely, sometimes tiresome, and even mundane. Hours away from family to shine a light for people that the keeper may never meet. The keeper had thought of quitting, but wondered what to do, where to go. I mean the keeper had been doing this for years. Locals knew the keeper and what it was the keeper did. The keeper though began to grow slack in the duties and responsibilities of the job. One particular night the keeper noticed that the light was dimming. Knowing what to do was not the issue. It was wanting to do it that was the problem. So, the keeper decided that it was not busy on this night, and it would not hurt for the light to dim. Next the keeper decided to sleep the rest of the night away. As morning arose the keeper made way to the boat to return home. Approaching the beach instantly the keeper spotted wreckage of their personal family boat. The keeper rushed to check with tears flowing and heart pounding, but it was too late. The keepers' family had decided to give a surprise visit that night and trusted that the light would be burning. Unfortunately, it was not. You see this is the story of the keeper of God's light. Sometimes you may feel like the lighthouse keeper in this story, but please never let your light go out. Because if your light goes out it will not just affect you. It can affect all those around you.

Mat 5:14-16 KJV 14 Ye are the light of the world. A city that is set on an hill cannot be hid. 15 Neither do men light a candle, and put it under a bushel, but on a candlestick; and it giveth light unto all that are in the house. 16 Let your light so shine before men, that they may see your good works, and glorify your Father which is in heaven.

LXIV.

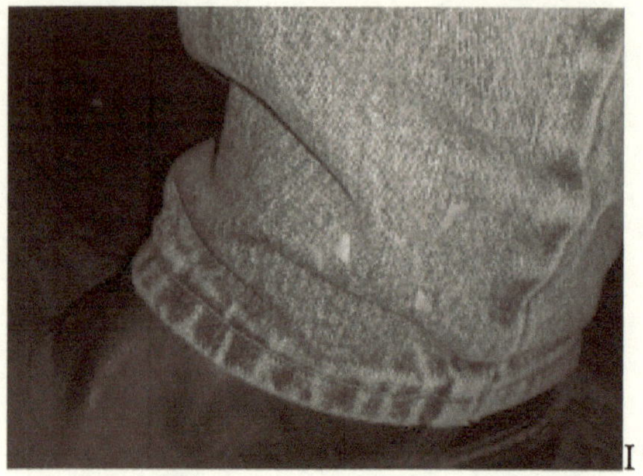

I was working on a project around the house one day. At some point I looked down, and I saw something all over my pants leg. There seemed to be hundreds of them. I've always called them hitchhikers; I'm sure different parts of the country call them different things. I stopped the project and started pulling them off. I got so consumed by them that I didn't realize how long I had been working on it. I finally said you know what I'll get them when I'm done with the project. Too often we are living for God and trying to do His will and we get distracted by something. We get caught up trying to fix this nuisance that we lose track of time. We need to prioritize what needs to be done and what can wait. Let us run the race and live for God to the fullest.

Hebrews 12:1 WEB Therefore let's also, seeing we are surrounded by so great a cloud of witnesses, lay aside every weight and the sin which so easily entangles us, and let's run with perseverance the race that is set before us,

LXV.

You hear people say all the time, strive to be great. I understand the thought, but in your striving to be great don't forget to be good. Being a good person makes you great. Because greatness doesn't mean rich and famous, it means being the best you can be at what you do. If you work for minimum wage or if you make millions of dollars, be great at what you do. That is greatness. Be good to people, respect people. I remember my dad and uncle were not rich people, but they were very respected and to the people that knew them they were great. I'm sure you have people in your life that come to mind just like this. People that didn't seek to be rich and famous. They were just good people. Those will be the people you remember forever. So, strive to be good, be the best you can, that is great.

Gal 6:9 ISV Let's not get tired of doing what is good, for at the right time we will reap a harvest—if we do not give up.

LXVI.

When I was in high school, we had an individual come and speak to us. I would like to share in essence the thought that he shared. Imagine if you will, that you have a certain possession, say a tool, gaming system, a nice car, whatever it may be. You would strive to take care of these things, as you should. You wouldn't want anything to happen to them to damage them by you or anyone else. Now imagine how mad you would be if something did happen to your prized possession. How often, though, do we harm those around us or see others harm them and it doesn't affect us. As this person told us years ago, we love things and use people when we should love people and use things. So, let's make sure we are loving people and using things.

Joh 13:34-35 ISV 34 I'm giving you a new commandment...to love one another. Just as I have loved you, you also should love one another. 35 This is how everyone will know that you are my disciples, if you have love for one another."

LXVII.

You sit down to put a puzzle together, and you're almost done. Then you realize that there is a piece missing. You search the box, you look under the table, you try and try. Unfortunately, it's just not there. You don't try to fill the empty spot with something else though, because it just wouldn't be right. Some out there are searching for something to fill a hole in their soul. The problem is the hole is a God shaped hole, and there is nothing else that will fill it. They may say that they don't need Jesus, or they don't need more of Jesus. I was once the person that thought the same way. I can tell you from experience that you'll spend a lot of time and effort trying to fill this hole with anything other than Jesus. You may jump from job to job, relationship to relationship. You may start trying to fill it with entertainment, fun, alcohol, drugs. There may be no end, but it'll never be right. Not until you fill it with Jesus. Do that today, quit looking for fulfillment in everything else. Allow Jesus to make you whole.

1 Thessalonians 5:23 MSG

23 May God himself, the God who makes everything holy and whole, make you holy and whole, put you together - spirit, soul, and body - and keep you fit for the coming of our Master, Jesus Christ.

LXVIII.

Imagine you are watching a race where one of the racers keeps falling. They keep getting back up and trying again. Before long you and everyone else watching would begin to cheer them on. While you are trying to walk with God and you have something you can't seem to overcome, know this. Everybody has something they battle with. Whatever it may be, everyone has it. You struggle with it and say to yourself never again. I'm not doing this ever again, but you do. You fall flat on your face. This is where you get back up. You see falling does not make you evil, it makes you human. You just have to get back up. Don't let that thing you battle stop you from living for God. You will eventually conquer this. He will forgive, he is our father, and He will help you. My children may do things I dislike, but it does not change the love I have for them, and neither will your problem cause God to not love you. So don't stay down, get up and try again. Finish the race.

Pro 24:16 KJV For a just man falleth seven times, and riseth up again: but the wicked shall fall into mischief.

LXIX.

The thought came to me that we invest a lot of time and effort into things that are important to us. We go to school for years. We study countless hours, spend crazy amounts in classes and books to learn a trade. We get in our trade and get busy with life and realize that we have money now so we can afford to eat more. We eat more and suddenly we're out of shape. So, we get a gym membership, go after work and our days off to exercise. We buy healthier, more expensive food. Then we study all the ways to get in shape. Then one day somebody asks us about retirement. Wow, we hadn't even thought about that. Then you study what's the best way to save for retirement. Then we spend many years saving, planning, and dreaming of one day finally retiring. We spend all this time and effort into these things, and I'm not saying we shouldn't. What I'm saying is how much time do we invest into where we will spend eternity? Do we study the Bible, go to church to learn more about Jesus and eternity? Do we talk to Jesus and seek His will for our lives? Should we not be investing real time, effort and thought into eternity?

Matthew 6:20 KJV But lay up for yourselves treasures in heaven, where neither moth nor rust doth corrupt, and where thieves do not break through nor steal: 21. For where your treasure is, there will your heart be also.

LXX.

I heard on the radio that people have said in a survey that if they lost their phones, they would pay more than $1000 to get their phones back. Not just any phone but their phone, with all their information. So, this gave me a thought. I know that people go frantic if they lose their phones. They will get help from anybody nearby even if they are strangers. The lengths someone is willing to go through to get their phones back are astounding. The question is, why is it we don't put the same energy when we find ourselves drifting from God. Ask yourself this question, apply it to your life. Because God is the single most important thing you could ever have in your life. Draw near to God, and he will draw near to you.

Mar 12:29-30 KJV 29 And Jesus answered him, The first of all the commandments is, Hear, O Israel; The Lord our God is one Lord: 30 And thou shalt love the Lord thy God with all thy heart, and with all thy soul, and with all thy mind, and with all thy strength: this is the first commandment.

LXXI.

I got to see a sight that you don't get to see regularly. I was on top of a structure and saw the top side of fog. This view prompted a thought. You see if you're driving through this, you'd barely be able to see. You may have to drive slowly, squint your eyes, and pray you don't wreck. From above though I could see clearly. Sometimes in life you may not be able to see clearly, it may be "foggy". You may wonder what's going on or if you will ever get out of this. Just remember God is above the troubles in your life and can see clearly. He will bring you through it. So, squint your eyes if you have to, go slow if needed. Just keep believing that God is watching over you.

Mat 14:29-31 KJV 29 And he said, Come. And when Peter was come down out of the ship, he walked on the water, to go to Jesus. 30 But when he saw the wind boisterous, he was afraid; and beginning to sink, he cried, saying, Lord, save me. 31 And immediately Jesus stretched forth his hand, and caught him, and said unto him, O thou of little faith, wherefore didst thou doubt?

LXXII.

We are forgiven because of the sacrifice that Jesus made for us. We receive and enjoy forgiveness. Everyone likes to be forgiven, but we don't so much enjoy forgiving. We feel like we have a right to hold onto a grudge or offense. I mean if someone has wronged us, shouldn't we have the right to stay angry with them or hold it against them. The problem with that is when I think about how much Jesus has forgiven me what right do I have to not forgive someone else. We want to learn to be like Jesus, but when presented with the opportunity to forgive, we want to handle it our way. We want to tell that person off, set them straight, and let them know that they don't know who they are messing with. Didn't Jesus tell his disciples to forgive 490 times a day? Are you going to get offended? Yes. Do you have a right to defend yourself? Again, yes. Do you have the right to not forgive? Well, Jesus says in Matthew if we don't forgive others, He will not forgive us. Now, if you can live with that, be my guest, but I don't want me not forgiving someone to stop me from being forgiven. I just ask if you read this, apply it to your own life. Live willing to forgive others when needed because we have been forgiven so much.

Mat 6:12-15 ISV 12 and forgive us our sins, as we have forgiven those who have sinned against us. 13 And never bring us into temptation, but deliver us from the evil one.' 14 Because if you forgive people their offenses, your heavenly Father will also forgive you. 15 But if you do not forgive people their offenses, your Father will not forgive your offenses."

LXXIII.

My wife was at a doctor's appointment once. She had already been brought to the back and placed in a room. She had been there for quite some time, so she stepped out to see what was going on. When she did, the Doctor saw her and said "Oh, I forgot you were in there." Obviously, this upset my wife because of the time wasted, and nobody wants to be forgotten.

Mat 1:3 KJV And Judas begat Phares and Zara of Thamar; and Phares begat Esrom; and Esrom begat Aram;

Mat 1:6 KJV And Jesse begat David the king; and David the king begat Solomon of her that had been the wife of Urias;

Zara and Uriah had no place in the lineage of Christ. They were not ancestors of Christ. Zara's place as the firstborn had been taken by Phares (Genesis 38:28-30). Uriah's wife had been taken by David. Then Uriah was set up to die. They had been done wrong. Even sinned against. God never mentions the wrongdoing or David's sin. He did mention the ones who had been wronged. I think sometimes we feel like if God forgives someone and forgets their sin or wrongdoing against us, that in turn he also forgets us. I think that these two are mentioned to point out to us that God does not forget us, be it a small thing or a large thing done against us. God has not forgotten us nor will He.

Isa 49:15 NHEB "Can a woman forget her nursing child, that she should not have compassion on the son of her womb? Yes, these may forget, yet I will not forget you.

LXXIV.

Have you ever known someone who stayed in an abusive relationship? They might decide to leave it, but go right back to it, or even another one just like it. Most of us have had the conversation wondering why people stay in these relationships. All the while many people today walk around in a very similar relationship with fear. People hold onto their fear like they will lose part of themselves if they let it go. Like they won't be able to make it without it. Or they are so used to it, they don't even realize how bad it is. Fear has many names and takes many shapes and sizes. It may be anxiety, panic attacks, the fear that something terrible will happen, or whatever it may be. It's time to walk away from fear, we don't have to tolerate it. We can live life without constant fear. God didn't give it to you so don't keep it, get your freedom.

2Timothy 1:7 KJV For God hath not given us the spirit of fear; but of power, and of love, and of a sound mind.

LXXV.

When you have a new baby, you love them dearly, and you love them just like they are. That being said, because you love them you don't want them to stay the way they are. You want them to grow, you want them to be able to feed themselves, you want them to be able to eat solid food, you want them to learn to potty on their own, you want them to learn to talk, you want them to learn to dress themselves, you want them to go to school and learn more, you want them to have discipline, you want them to mature. You see you love them, and because of that, you want them to change. I've often heard it said, "God loves us just the way we are, but He loves us too much to leave us that way." Living for God requires us to change. We have to allow God to make the changes in us that he wants.

2 Corinthians 5:17 KJV Therefore if any man be in Christ, he is a new creature: old things are passed away; behold, all things are become new.

LXXVI.

Imagine you have a toddler, and they played outside all day. As the day winds down it's time to go inside, but they are having too much fun to want to go in. They may even say that they never want to go inside. Obviously, as a loving parent you're not going to cave to their demands and just let them stay outside like this. You finally get them inside, and now it's time for supper and a bath. Well, they don't want supper, they want to play. They finally yield and eat, not realizing how hungry they were. Then the bath and another battle because they don't want to. Yet again, as a loving parent you know they need to be clean. So, they get their bath and by this time they have little energy left to fight bedtime. As they doze off to sleep you stand there looking at this child that you love so much.

This is a reflection of how God is and often how we respond. God wants to take us out of this world of sin, but we're having too much fun. We fight God when as a loving Father, He is trying to take care of us. When He finally gets us in, He feeds us and cleans us from the sin in our lives. Sometimes we resist this process wanting to hold onto part of the world. Then when we finally yield, we get to rest peacefully as God looks on. Today, if God has been dealing with you, don't fight Him anymore. He loves you and just wants to take care of you.

Psalm 103:13: "The Lord is like a father to his children, tender and compassionate to those who fear him."

Luke 11:13 BBE If, then, you who are evil are able to give good things to your children, how much more will your Father in heaven give the Holy Spirit to those who make request to him?

LXXVII.

Have you ever had to buy a storage building or rent a storage unit? If so, it's because you began to accumulate more stuff than you had room for. Then, we get more stuff. Eventually we decide there is a need to get rid of some stuff. Or we decide we have to move, then we have to pack stuff, have a garage sale, and then just toss a bunch of stuff that we've accumulated over the years. We often do this in our walk with God. We start picking up stuff along the way that we don't need. All it does is cause clutter and slow us down. It can trip us up and be harmful to our walk with God. So, let's do some spiritual spring cleaning. Let's look through our lives and see if we have stuff that isn't helping us and needs to go.

Heb 12:1-2 KJV 1 Wherefore seeing we also are compassed about with so great a cloud of witnesses, let us lay aside every weight, and the sin which doth so easily beset us, and let us run with patience the race that is set before us, 2 Looking unto Jesus the author and finisher of our faith; who for the joy that was set before him endured the cross, despising the shame, and is set down at the right hand of the throne of God.

LXXVIII.

I remember my daddy telling me the story of his little brother, my Uncle Fred, following him around in the woods. They came upon some mayhaws. My uncle, seeing how pretty they were, asked my dad if they were good to eat. Being the prankster that he was, my dad told him yes. My uncle then grabs a handful and throws him in his mouth. This is when he discovered that mayhaws are not naturally sweet but bitter. They make great jellies, but you gotta add a lot of sugar. Now this was a funny story to hear growing up. Today, it provokes a thought. We as Christians are not supposed to be bitter.

Amos 6:12 BBE Is it possible for horses to go running on the rock? may the sea be ploughed with oxen? for the right to be turned by you into poison, and the fruit of righteousness into a bitter plant?

Is it possible for the fruit of righteousness to be in a bitter plant? That's the question posed here

Heb 12:14-15 KJV 14 Follow peace with all men, and holiness, without which no man shall see the Lord: 15 Looking diligently lest any man fail of the grace of God; lest any root of bitterness springing up trouble you, and thereby many be defiled;

Jas 3:11-18 KJV 11 Doth a fountain send forth at the same place sweet water and bitter? 12 Can the fig tree, my brethren, bear olive berries? either a vine, figs? so can no fountain both yield salt water and fresh. 13 Who is a wise man and endued with knowledge among you? let him shew out of a good conversation his works with meekness of wisdom. 14 But if ye have bitter envying and strife in your hearts, glory not, and lie not against the truth. 15 This wisdom descendeth not from above, but is earthly, sensual, devilish. 16 For where envying and strife is, there is confusion and every evil work. 17 But the wisdom that is from above is first pure, then peaceable, gentle, and easy to be intreated, full of mercy and good fruits, without partiality, and without hypocrisy. 18 And the fruit of righteousness is sown in peace of them that make peace.

You want the fruit of righteousness? Make peace. Don't be bitter, but instead be merciful and forgiving.

LXXIX.

You ever do something that you felt like you deserved more attention for. You may have done something extra at work or at home. You may have gone out of your way to help someone. Or maybe you got a really special gift for someone, and they barely even thanked you. I wonder how Jesus feels when He gave his life for us, and we often don't even give him much attention. I'd like to dive into His sacrifice a little.

Isa 53:3-5 KJV 3 He is despised and rejected of men; a man of sorrows, and acquainted with grief: and we hid as it were our faces from him; he was despised, and we esteemed him not. 4 Surely he hath borne our griefs, and carried our sorrows: yet we did esteem him stricken, smitten of God, and afflicted. 5 But he was wounded for our transgressions, he was bruised for our iniquities: the chastisement of our peace was upon him; and with his stripes we are healed.

Most of us are familiar with this scripture. Have we ever stopped and really thought about it? Let's read a couple different translations.

Isaiah 53:3 NLT

3 He was despised and rejected. a man of sorrows, acquainted with deepest grief. We turned our backs on him and looked the other way. He was despised, and we did not care.

Isa 53:3 Easy English People did not like him. And they caused him to go away. He was a man who often felt very sad. And he knew what pain felt like. He was like someone that people hid their faces from. People did not like him. And we decided that he was not worth anything.

People did not like Him. They caused Him to go away, hid their faces and decided that He wasn't worth anything. It's heartbreaking to think that Jesus was thought of this way, but what's more heartbreaking is that He still is. After all that He has done for us all, taking on the punishment for our sins, receiving stripes for our healing, and yet he is still treated this way. We need to question ourselves and make sure that we don't reject Him. We need to be careful that we don't put our relationship with Jesus on the back burner, not giving it our full attention. After all, it was us He gave His life for. Shouldn't we live for Him?

LXXX.

I asked my children a question once. I asked how much poop would be an acceptable amount to put in your food. The look of disgust on their faces as they piped up "none." I then began to ask why then is it okay to put garbage into our spiritual diets with what we watch or listen to?

Rom 1:29-32 ISV 29 They have become filled with every kind of wickedness, evil, greed, and depravity. They are full of envy, murder, quarreling, deceit, and viciousness. They are gossips, 30 slanderers, God-haters, haughty, arrogant, boastful, inventors of evil, disobedient to their parents, 31 foolish, faithless, heartless, and ruthless. 32 Although they know God's just requirement—that those who practice such things deserve to die—they not only do these things but even applaud others who practice them.

We read this scripture and amen it. We think how evil these things are. Yet we bypass the very last part where it says even applaud others who practice them. Don't we do that though? We watch whatever we want for entertainment, not considering that we are applauding those very things. We really need to pay close attention to what we put in front of our eyes for entertainment as it says in:

Psalm101:3 KJV I will set no wicked thing before mine eyes: I hate the work of them that turn aside; it shall not cleave to me.

You can actually read Psalm 101 and most of the chapter can apply to what we watch and allow in our homes. There's your homework: go read Psalm 101 and pray for God to give you direction. Let's not put trash into our spiritual diets.

LXXXI.

Have you ever felt ignored? It may have been from a spouse or close friend. It may have not been intentional. They may have gotten busy with their day and simply forgot to respond to your texts. You may have been somewhere in public, and the other seemed to be more into conversations with everyone else but you. Even though it's unintentional, it still can bother you. Or maybe you were the one doing the ignoring. Now I'm not saying that we don't get busy with our day-to-day activities. I understand that sometimes that happens. If, though, it's a continuous habit then it can be harmful to your relationship. The Bible says in 1 Thessalonians 5:17 Pray without ceasing. Other words, be in constant communication with God. How often do we ignore God all day, then right at the end try to squeeze in a few minutes with Him or worse yet only talk to Him at church? Our relationship with God will suffer just like our earthly relationships will if we have a constant lack of communication.

Mat 6:33 KJV But seek ye first the kingdom of God, and his righteousness; and all these things shall be added unto you.

Mar 12:29-30 KJV 29 And Jesus answered him, The first of all the commandments is, Hear, O Israel; The Lord our God is one Lord: 30 And thou shalt love the Lord thy God with all thy heart, and with all thy soul, and with all thy mind, and with all thy strength: this is the first commandment.

LXXXII.

In military training, soldiers are put to the ultimate tests. They are taught to push themselves to the limits. The punishment their minds and bodies are put through only make them stronger for what they may face. The trials they go through are not meant to break them, but to push them past their breaking point so that they can endure the battle. We, too, as soldiers in the Lord's army, go through many things, but they are not meant to destroy us. Rather, they are meant to strengthen us. The trials build our endurance so that we may withstand it. So, if you've done all to stand. Stand!

2Ti 2:3 KJV Thou therefore endure hardness, as a good soldier of Jesus

LXXXIII.

I was at church one day when no one was there so there were no lights on. I had walked into the sanctuary and noticed the exit sign shining above the door. I couldn't see the door because of how dark it was, which is why there is an exit sign shining brightly in the darkness to show the safe way out. As Christians, it is our job to shine brightly in this dark world to show the safe way out of the darkness. If our light isn't shining brightly, how will people know the way? So, draw closer to Jesus and let His light shine brightly through you.

1Pe 2:9 KJV But ye are a chosen generation, a royal priesthood, an holy nation, a peculiar people; that ye should shew forth the praises of him who hath called you out of darkness into his marvellous light:

Mat 5:16 KJV Let your light so shine before men, that they may see your good works, and glorify your Father which is in heaven.

LXXXIV.

The term "strike while the iron is hot" comes from a blacksmith striking a horseshoe or other piece of metal when the temperature of the metal was exactly right. If the blacksmith would wait too long, then the metal would cool and become more difficult to shape. Sometimes we may be in a service where God is really moving on us. We feel the tug of the Spirit. Yet we pull back and walk away, resisting the conviction placed upon us. If we wait too long, just like the iron, we may become too difficult to shape. Don't be like Felix, who told Paul to come back at a more convenient time. (Acts 24:25). We never hear of Felix calling Paul again. Strike while the iron is hot. Change as soon as the LORD calls.

1Th 5:19 KJV Quench not the Spirit.

1Th 5:19 ISV Do not put out the Spirit's fire.

LXXXV.

A coworker told me a story once about a splinter he had gotten. He said that he was sitting at desk and felt something in his hand. He began to squeeze it and out popped a splinter. An infection had set around it and had forced it out. He began to try and remember getting this splinter. That's when it dawned on him that it was many years prior that it had happened. He remembered getting it and had tried to remove it, but it was too deep. So, he just left it, thinking it'll work its way out. It took many years, but it did. We too have things that work their way into our lives that harm us. A "thorn" in the flesh if you will as Paul had in 2 Cor 12:7-9. We try to remove it, but sometimes that just isn't going to happen. It may be too deep. Eventually, like my coworker, it just becomes part of our life. We just keep moving through our day-to-day living. We may even forget about it. Eventually, it becomes infected and works its way to the surface where we have to deal with it. Now, though, it's gone, we are healed of this hurt, though it may leave a scar. It may take time, but how do we deal with it until then? God's grace.

2Co 12:9 KJV And he said unto me, My grace is sufficient for thee: for my strength is made perfect in weakness. Most gladly therefore will I rather glory in my infirmities, that the power of Christ may rest upon me.

LXXXVI.

You know when you're driving down the road and you see road signs with arrows letting you know that there is a curve up ahead? You know they are there for your protection and to give you direction. Just like guardrails on bridges, stop signs, and other road signs. You see God will also guide us in the way that we should go if we are attentive. Just like these road signs aren't trying to keep you from enjoying yourself, neither is God. He really wants what's best for you. For that to happen you have to follow the path He directs you to take.

Psa 119:35 NHEB Direct me in the path of your commandments, for I delight in them.

LXXXVII.

Have you ever been working with someone at night, and they have a flashlight or headlamp that they can't seem to keep out of your face? It can get very irritating. Plus, if it's already dark and they shine their light in your eyes now you are seeing worse than you were before. We have to make sure when we are shining our light before men, that we are doing it in love. Because if we, do it any other way, we may just be shining it in their face. Instead of trying to help them see we may end up blinding them.

Mat 5:16 NET In the same way, let your light shine before people, so that they can see your good deeds and give honor to your Father in heaven.

1Co 16:14 ISV Everything you do should be done lovingly.

LXXXVIII.

Have you ever heard about someone that had a praying mama, daddy, or grandparent? Whoever it may have been, they knew how to pray and touch God. I've heard stories of people that waited to go into battle until their mama was praying. Maybe you don't have somebody like this in your life. Well, I've got good news. You can be that somebody. You can be a prayer warrior. You can touch God with your prayers. I also want to bring something to your attention. Did you know that Jesus prayed for us? In John chapter 17. If I feel like I'm not going to make it, I will call on this prayer to keep me. Also, keep in mind that He is our advocate. So, if you are feeling down, remember Jesus prayed for you.

John 17:20 KJV Neither pray I for these alone, but for them also which shall believe on me through their word;

1Jn 2:1 KJV My little children, these things write I unto you, that ye sin not. And if any man sin, we have an advocate with the Father, Jesus Christ the righteous:

LXXXIX.

Was it morning or evening for you when you got that call? It may have been both, it may have been midnight. You know the call because your heart feels it right now as you read these words. Tears may even well up in your eyes. That loved one you will never see again. For me it's been a few calls. By far the worst was losing my nephew Tracey at 23 years old. I could barely get the words out of my mouth. The family and the church pulled together in support of my dear sister in her time of loss. Most of all, God was there. Healing has taken time, and there are still times that you just suddenly begin to cry. (I've often heard that tears are words that the heart and mouth can't express). The comment was made at his wake that it would be a bigger miracle to heal all the broken hearts left behind than to have raised him back to life. Yet, through this tragedy there will come times that we can reach out to others and help comfort them. It may be a hug, a prayer, a pat on the shoulder or tears shared together. We will be able to share the comfort that God has given us with others. You can do the same with the tragedies and heartaches you have endured. If you are going through loss, let Jesus wrap His arms around you and heal your heart.

2Co 1:4 BBE Who gives us comfort in all our troubles, so that we may be able to give comfort to others who are in trouble, through the comfort with which we ourselves are comforted by God.

XC.

Expanded metal is a metal produced from a solid metal sheet. You only need a small piece of metal for this process. The sheet goes through a process of cutting and stretching using industrial machinery. Stretching and cutting result in a mesh with diamond-shaped spaces. Many other patterns can also be created. Examples of metals used to make expanded metal include aluminum, stainless and galvanized steel, copper, and titanium. There are several types of expanded metal. Each type is made in different ways that provide various functions. The ratio of open to close mesh area specifies the amount of space for the passage of light, air, and water. The ratio can be changed according to the mesh usage. The process starts with a small sheet of steel and results in the production of a large mesh. The versatility of expanded metal widens the opportunity for usage. It can be used for a variety of applications. While still allowing airflow and light in, expanded metal is very strong and durable.

We need to be like expanded metal. Let God stretch us and cut out anything that would stop us from being what we are intended to be. We are all different, we're made of different materials. God can use our unique makeup to create us into a useful instrument in His kingdom. We have to let God's light shine through us and the Spirit to flow through us. You don't have to be great and well known for God to use. He starts with the small. We are made to stretch. Let us become strong and durable like expanded metal.

Jer 18:6 KJV O house of Israel, cannot I do with you as this potter? saith the LORD. Behold, as the clay is in the potter's hand, so are ye in mine hand, O house of Israel.

XCI.

If you're anything like me, you grew up with home remedies. Daddy always said that turpentine off of a pine tree can heal some wounds and pull-out infection. My uncle once had me boil an onion and give the water out of the pot with sugar in it to a gassy baby, and hey, it worked. The point is there are many things we can do at home, so we don't have to go to the emergency room or doctor. We can handle it at home. You know if you have a sickness or situation, you can pray the prayer of faith yourself. You don't always have to call the preacher or send out a prayer request to everyone. You can touch God. Now, there is nothing wrong at all with getting others to pray with you. You just need to know that you can pray about it and get an answer or a healing. In Mark 16 it says these signs shall follow them that believe. Do you believe? Then that's you. You can pray and touch God at home.

Mar 16:17-18 KJV 17 And these signs shall follow them that believe; In my name shall they cast out devils; they shall speak with new tongues; 18 They shall take up serpents; and if they drink any deadly thing, it shall not hurt them; they shall lay hands on the sick, and they shall recover.

XCII.

I was praying for a person once that was very ill and felt impressed by God, that sometimes it's just their time to die. So, I began to pray God's will be done and comfort for the family. We don't like to hear that, but sometimes it's just simply their time. Don't be discouraged if you pray and pray for someone and they don't recover. It may be that it was their time. I remember when my daddy was in the hospital and not doing well for a few months. I had prayed earnestly for my daddy because I loved him and didn't want to lose him. At some point in the hospital stay the Lord had assured me that my dad was going to be okay. A month later he passed. I was thinking God was going to heal him, but how much better is a healing that lets you be with Jesus. So don't think God isn't listening or doesn't care. Or you just didn't have enough faith. It may have been their appointed time.

Ecc 3:1-2 KJV 1 To every thing there is a season, and a time to every purpose under the heaven: 2 A time to be born, and a time to die; a time to plant, and a time to pluck up that which is planted;

XCIII.

Growing up my dad had quite a few fruit trees. He had different kinds of pears and plum trees. Do you know why the pear tree produced pears? It didn't produce pears because it was trying to prove it was a pear tree. It produced pears because it was a pear tree. We as Christians don't try to produce fruit to prove we are a Christian. We do it because we are Christians. So, dig your roots in, get fertilized in the soil of the LORD and produce fruit.

Gal 5:22-23 KJV 22 But the fruit of the Spirit is love, joy, peace, longsuffering, gentleness, goodness, faith, 23 Meekness, temperance: against such there is no law.

XCIV.

Addiction is rampant in our world today. People are addicted to drugs, alcohol, sugar, food, entertainment, cellphones. The things they are addicted to are the things they invest their money in. They spend time with their addiction. Sometimes the addiction separates them from the rest of the world. The Word of God talks about Stephanus being addicted to the ministry of the saints. Oh, that we would get addicted to the things of God. We would put our time, our effort and money into the kingdom. We would come out from the world and be separate. How better off we would be to let this be our addiction!

1Co 16:15 KJV I beseech you, brethren, (ye know the house of Stephanas, that it is the firstfruits of Achaia, and that they have addicted themselves to the ministry of the saints,)

XCV.

So, what do you see here? A tile floor, but what you probably first noticed is what was wrong. The tiles are missing. I, like you, would see the same thing and think well that needs to be fixed, and it does. What we don't even think about is the 4 to 6 inches concrete that's underneath is in good shape. It's holding us up, it's holding the building up. We don't see the good, only the flaws. We don't see the work that has already been done, nor do we see the potential. We look at ourselves and others the same way. We see the flaws and the shortcomings. God looks on the heart though. He sees the potential. Don't look down on yourself or others. Pray that God could help you see situations and people the way he does. Look for the good.

1Sa 16:7 KJV But the LORD said unto Samuel, Look not on his countenance, or on the height of his stature; because I have refused him: for the LORD seeth not as man seeth; for man looketh on the outward appearance, but the LORD looketh on the heart.

XCVI.

There are four main blood types: A, B, AB, and O. If someone has type A blood, they can only receive type A or type O blood. They cannot receive type B or type AB blood. If someone has type B blood, they can only receive type B or type O blood. They cannot receive type A or type AB blood. If someone has type AB blood, they can receive all blood types. If someone has type O blood, they can only receive type O blood. Now you may be thinking, why are we going over blood types? Well, I'll tell you. There are some people that only certain people can reach because they aren't compatible with others. There may be someone that you are in contact with that your neighbor at church or a preacher cannot reach. You might be able to, though. Sometimes people's experiences and personalities are compatible, and sometimes they aren't. Look around in your circle of people that you are in contact with. Pay attention because you may be a compatible "blood donor," that can introduce them to Jesus.

Pro 11:30 KJV The fruit of the righteous is a tree of life; and he that winneth souls is wise.

XCVII.

Anybody that knows me, knows that I am a coffee drinker. There is a lot to be said about a good cup of coffee. There is also plenty to be said about a bad cup. I have drunk coffee with people or tasted coffee that folks have made that was nasty. Usually when you take a sip of coffee you have to take a second sip to determine if it was as bad as I thought it was. And sometimes it is as bad as you thought it was or maybe even worse. I have had a couple cups of coffee that when I went to take a sip, I spit it back in the cup because it was that bad. When you get a good cup of coffee, though, a good cup of coffee is amazing. I have had people tell me that they didn't care for coffee, but they in turn tell me that they really like my coffee. You see often it's not the coffee but the maker or the presenter if you will. Now that being said, you may have got a bad taste of Jesus from someone. That does not mean that Jesus isn't good. It could just mean that whoever presented him to you did it incorrectly. If you have a bad taste in your mouth over Jesus, then taste again. If you have never tried Jesus, taste and see. Jesus is good and you can trust him.

Psalm 34:8 O taste and see that the LORD is good: blessed is the man that trusteth in him.

XCVIII.

You know if you decide you're going to build muscle mass you are going to have to work for it. You know that it's just not going to happen without it. You have to cut things out of your diet and replace them with things that will help build muscle. You've got to exercise. You may start out lifting 50 pounds, but if you're going to build more muscle you are going to have to lift more weight. You can't just lift 50 pounds every day and expect to all of a sudden lift 300 pounds. When you do begin to lift more, you actually begin to cause tiny tears in your muscles which are called micro tears. The body repairs this and adapts to better handle the resistance caused by the damage. I have heard it this way, you have to break the muscle down to build it back stronger. Many people commit to this process, but when it gets harder, and it will get harder, they quit. They just weren't ready to make the sacrifices necessary to make it work. The same concept applies to having faith. It's not just going to happen. If we want more faith, then we've got to cut some things out and replace them with things that will build our faith. We've got to exercise our faith. We will have to deal with bigger problems and heavier things that will increase our faith. If we only ever deal with 50-pound problems, we most likely will not be prepared to handle a 300-pound problem. Sometimes in the stretching, there will be tearing, and we may even have a breakdown in faith. This, however, will make our faith come back stronger. God is our personal trainer, and as a personal trainer, He knows exactly what each of us needs to build our faith. Don't lose heart, and don't quit just because it gets hard, and it will. Press on and build your faith.

1Ti 4:8 KJV For bodily exercise profiteth little: but godliness is profitable unto all things, having promise of the life that now is, and of that which is to come.

Jas 2:17-18 KJV 17 Even so faith, if it hath not works, is dead, being alone. 18 Yea, a man may say, Thou hast faith, and I have works:

shew me thy faith without thy works, and I will shew thee my faith by my works.

XCIX.

My little boy got a glow stick in a goody bag, and he was complaining that it didn't work. He had already turned all the lights off to play with it. What he didn't understand is it had to be broken to shine its light. Don't be surprised in your walk with God that you go through a breaking. Nobody likes to be broken, but we all want to shine brighter. Sometimes we will have to go through the breaking process to become more like Jesus. So be patient in the process, it will make you shine brighter.

Mat 5:16 KJV Let your light so shine before men, that they may see your good works, and glorify your Father which is in heaven.

C.

I cannot tell you how many times that I have asked my kids what the thermostat is set at. What I hear most of the time is which number is it or they would just read the temperature. I then explain to them again that the big number is the temperature of the room. What I want to know is what the temperature is set at. If I'm asking this question, it's because I don't like the temperature the room is, and I want to change it. We need to be thermostats and not just thermometers. We don't just need to read the temperature in our lives and its situations. We need to be able to adjust the temperature or way things are headed. When Jesus entered a room, things changed. Let's be those who change the feel of a room for the better when we enter it.

Romans 12:2 NLT

2 Don't copy the behavior and customs of this world, but let God transform you into a new person by changing the way you think. Then you will learn to know God's will for you, which is good and pleasing and perfect.

CI.

Have you ever heard a story about a car accident or a crime that took place? Then when the police arrive everybody says they didn't see anything. They were witnesses, they just didn't want to say what it was they witnessed for whatever reason. Have you ever prayed for God to make you a witness? Well, I want to let you know that you are witnesses, that is a given. A good witness or a bad one, that is the question. Paul said it this way "you are epistles." As I have heard it said: we are the only Bible some people will ever read. That being said, what are they reading? Let's make sure they are reading the right things that will lead them closer to Christ.

Isa 43:10 KJV Ye are my witnesses, saith the LORD, and my servant whom I have chosen: that ye may know and believe me, and understand that I am he: before me there was no God formed, neither shall there be after me.

Act 1:8 KJV But ye shall receive power, after that the Holy Ghost is come upon you: and ye shall be witnesses unto me both in Jerusalem, and in all Judaea, and in Samaria, and unto the uttermost part of the earth.

CII.

Distracted driving is dangerous. Be it because you're sleepy, messing with your phone, or whatever you may be doing. Being distracted while driving could harm you and bystanders. Just like in the natural, being distracted in the spiritual can be dangerous. While we travel this straight and narrow way, let us make sure that we don't become distracted. There are many things trying to catch our attention and get us off the path. If we get too distracted, we could cause spiritual harm to us and others. So, let's stay focused on the path in front of us and keep moving forward.

Pro 4:25-27 BBE 25 Keep your eyes on what is in front of you, looking straight before you. 26 Keep a watch on your behaviour; let all your ways be rightly ordered. 27 Let there be no turning to the right or to the left, keep your feet from evil.

CIII.

My daddy "Big John" was a pig farmer in the latter part of his life. I don't know how many people I saw come through there to buy hogs. I do remember one man, though. I don't remember his name, but I do remember the story. He was an older black gentleman, and someone had given him a ride to our place so he could buy some hogs. Daddy had built raised sides on his truck so he could haul hogs. He had agreed to haul the hogs for the man, so we loaded them in the back of daddy's truck. We stood there for a while waiting for the man's ride to come back and get him. Because it was taking so long the man asked Daddy if he could just ride with him. My dad said, "Why, sure". The man then reached to grab the rails to climb in the back of the truck. My Daddy quickly grabbed the man's arm and asked him what he was doing. "Well," the man said, "I didn't figure you would want me to ride in the front with y'all." My Daddy got visually upset. He responded to the man with something I've remembered my entire life. He said "Fella, you bought two hogs there, a white one and a black one. When you get home, you're going to butcher these hogs up. When you cut them open, you know what you're going to find on the inside? The same exact thing. Now get in the front of the truck." See Daddy understood something that some folks still don't understand, we're all the same. We have to love each other with no prejudices.

Heb 13:1 KJV Let brotherly love continue.

1Jn 4:20-21 KJV 20 If a man say, I love God, and hateth his brother, he is a liar: for he that loveth not his brother whom he hath seen, how can he love God whom he hath not seen? 21 And this commandment have we from him, That he who loveth God love his brother also.

CIV. Tools of the trade

Let's say you're working on a project, and you need to drive a nail. You send someone to get you something to drive the nail in. They return and have a saw in hand. At this point, an eye squint would set in your expression as you would be wondering, what am I supposed to do with that. You know you don't drive nails with saws, and you don't cut boards with hammers. We also have specialized tools that you may hardly ever pull out of the toolbox, but they do a job that they are tailored fitted for. You use the right tool for the job. We are God's tools to be used at the right time. You may not be a hammer; you may be a saw. Don't get discouraged because you can't do what someone else does. That may not be your use. You also may be a specialized tool that gets used in a different way that only you can do. It may be that one person that nobody else can reach that God has designed you to be able to do. So, focus on what you can do and be good at it. Be ready to be used when God needs you.

Phi 2:13 KJV For it is God which worketh in you both to will and to do of his good pleasure.

CV.

You remember the excitement of dating your spouse? Remember how you couldn't wait to talk to them, you almost counted the minutes until you could see them again. You planned the wedding, oh the time and effort, but it was all worth it. You're finally married, and you spend your first couple years in the state of adventure almost. However, as time goes on and it's just day to day living you begin to get bored. This is where it can get dangerous for some people. Some people will start looking for excitement in other places, not understanding that lack of excitement is not equivalent to lack of love. Not realizing that a relationship that is built on love and trust, or that it is built in the trenches of everyday life. Unfortunately, some will look to another person for this excitement and may even lose their relationship with their spouse due to this. Don't do this! Invest in your relationship with your spouse. Know that it may get "boring" but growing old together may be boring at times.

We often do this with our relationship with Jesus. Boy when we first get in, we are on fire, ready to take on the world. As days turn into months and months turn into years we tend to not invest as much into our spiritual life. We only spend church services communing with God rather than on a daily basis. Imagine if we only spent that much time with our spouse. We don't read the Bible, pray, and seek His face. We start looking for excitement or fulfillment in other places, often in entertainment. We spend hours on end watching almost anything when we should be spending time with Jesus. You ever wonder why it is called a walk with God? It's walking day in and day out. Stop looking in other places for your fulfillment, turn to Jesus and walk with Him.

Mic 6:8 WEB He has shown you, O man, what is good. What does Yahweh require of you, but to act justly, to love mercy, and to walk humbly with your God?

Rev 2:4 KJV Nevertheless I have somewhat against thee, because thou hast left thy first love.

CVI.

How often do we hear, man, I can't wait to go on vacation, I'd rather be anywhere but here? I'm ready for this thing or that thing. We're all waiting and wishing for the next big thing. Now I'm not saying there is anything wrong with vacations or wanting to go or here or there. What I'm saying is we have to learn to enjoy our life. Just day to day life. Because that will be the majority of our life. Not the vacations or the parties but the everyday going to work, having supper with family, being around the people in your life. Want your life to be more meaningful? Live for God, share His love and truth with others. Include God in your everyday life and enjoy it.

Heb 13:5 KJV Let your conversation be without covetousness; and be content with such things as ye have: for he hath said, I will never leave thee, nor forsake thee.

CVII.

You ever have a meal, let's say a burger, that you bought. And when it came out it was just a mess. The lettuce was hanging off, tomatoes falling out, with about as much mayo on the outside as there is on the inside. The presentation does not leave a very good impression. It may have tasted fine, but you could tell whoever did it, didn't care. I wonder sometimes if we present ourselves to God that way. We just show up for church ready to leave, plopping down on a pew and complaining about the music, the temperature, somebody else, whatever we can find. God is not the first thing on our mind. Now, we may get ourselves in order and get into service, but it takes a bit. Why not present ourselves better? Show up ready even though it's a sacrifice. Take the time to get in touch with God and stay in touch with him. Come to church expecting and excited for what God has in store, and then take what is given and use it in your day to day lives.

Rom 12:1 KJV I beseech you therefore, brethren, by the mercies of God, that ye present your bodies a living sacrifice, holy, acceptable unto God, which is your reasonable service.

CVIII. Safety First, Unless it's Second

That's a phrase I commonly use. I know managers and safety guys' heads will nearly explode when they see this, so let me explain. It is our nature as humans to take risks. That's why you asked that guy or girl out. That's why you have the job you have because we take risks. We are even taught to take risks like these, because you'll never hit the ball if you don't swing. Then there are other risks we take. We speed, don't wear seat belts, zip in and out of traffic. If it saves us time or makes it easier, it programs our brains to think it's good. Even managers and safety guys. I've seen it too many times. Now, I've never seen somebody purposely put someone in a dangerous situation. Either way. It's what we do as people. So why wouldn't we take risks for the kingdom? Are we afraid of what people might think of us? Shouldn't we be more afraid that they might die lost? Or honestly more concerned about what Jesus thinks of us. Your risk may be a ministry. It may be relocating to where God wants you like Abraham did. It may be increasing your giving. It may be talking to your coworkers about Jesus. Whatever the risk God is calling you to take, take it. Your brain will get programmed to see that it's good.

Dan 3:16-18 KJV 16 Shadrach, Meshach, and Abednego, answered and said to the king, O Nebuchadnezzar, we are not careful to answer thee in this matter. 17 If it be so, our God whom we serve is able to deliver us from the burning fiery furnace, and he will deliver us out of thine hand, O king. 18 But if not, be it known unto thee, O king, that we will not serve thy gods, nor worship the golden image which thou hast set up.

Act 5:28-29 KJV 28 Saying, Did not we straitly command you that ye should not teach in this name? and, behold, ye have filled Jerusalem with your doctrine, and intend to bring this man's blood upon us. 29 Then Peter and the other apostles answered and said, We ought to obey God rather than men.

CIX.

Uncle Fred had a little bit of a temper on him, to say the least. He once was working on a job where he was the head welder. He had trained a younger guy to weld. This guy was up on a structure welding when the safety man showed up. The safety man approached Uncle Fred and asked him if this guy was certified. Uncle Fred told the safety man that he certified him. Well, the safety man didn't like this, so he began to reprimand Uncle Fred. At this point Uncle Fred grabbed him by the collar and drug him over to the nearby lake. He pointed out and said, "You see that water? I'll pitch you right out in it." That was enough for the safety man. He hopped in his vehicle and left. You see he didn't have a fear of Uncle Fred until he got educated on it. I believe we as a whole have lost a healthy fear of God. How often do we tempt God's anger by our actions? Know that God loves us, and He is merciful. But we need not take His mercy for granted or see it as a license to sin. We should want to please our Father and, remember that He is a jealous God. We don't need to be doing the things everyone else does, but instead serve God faithfully and happily.

Pro 9:10 KJV The fear of the LORD is the beginning of wisdom: and the knowledge of the holy is understanding.

Deu 6:13-16 KJV 13 Thou shalt fear the LORD thy God, and serve him, and shalt swear by his name. 14 Ye shall not go after other gods, of the gods of the people which are round about you; 15 (For the LORD thy God is a jealous God among you) lest the anger of the LORD thy God be kindled against thee, and destroy thee from off the face of the earth. 16 Ye shall not tempt the LORD your God, as ye tempted him in Massah.

CX. A Dehydrated Soul

Our family made a trip to Disney World in June one year. You know June, one of the hottest months of the year. I told my family before we left that my goal was to keep them alive by keeping them hydrated. You see, I work in the elements year-round. I know what it's like to stay outside in the heat all day. I also know what dehydration can do. It can cause permanent damage and even death. Your body doesn't work right when you're dehydrated. You get very thirsty, which means you're already dehydrated. You often stop sweating, you may start stumbling, slurred speech is another symptom. Most people don't even realize that they are dehydrated until it's too late. Just like our physical body, we can dehydrate our spiritual body. If we aren't filling ourselves with Jesus, if we aren't reading His Word, we can become spiritually dehydrated. A person may not know until it's too late, so we have to watch for the symptoms. You may stop "sweating" or releasing salt, we are the salt of the earth. You may start stumbling more easily. You may have slurred speech, that is not clearly sharing Jesus. If we wait too long, we could even die spiritually. I do have to add, as being a husband and dad, it is our responsibility to make sure our family isn't spiritually dehydrated. So, let's drink the water that Jesus gives and teach our families to do the same.

Joh 4:14 ISV But whoever drinks the water that I will give him will never become thirsty again. The water that I will give him will become a well of water for him, springing up to eternal life."

Joh 7:37 ISV On the last and most important day of the festival, Jesus stood up and shouted, "If anyone is thirsty, let him come to me and drink!

CXI.

We've all done it, walked into a public bathroom and the smell hits you right in the face. You try to rush through getting your business done so you can escape the unbearable stench. By the time you leave the bathroom though it doesn't seem to stink as bad. You're slowly becoming used to the smell. Sin is the same way. When you first come in contact with it, you think "This is horrible". The longer you expose yourself to it, however, the less it bothers you. Eventually you barely even notice it if you notice it at all. So, separate yourself from anything that would cause you to become numb to sin.

2Co 6:17 BBE For which cause, Come out from among them, and be separate, says the Lord, and let no unclean thing come near you; and I will take you for myself,

CXII.

When my oldest son, Joshua, was a child I always told him that if you do something wrong come tell me. If you tell me, it'll be better than if I find out on my own. One such occasion arose. He was outside playing with a baseball. I had told him to stay away from the house and vehicles because I didn't want him to break anything. I was inside with my mama chatting when all of the sudden I heard this noise. Before I could make a few steps to investigate, my son burst in the door. He quickly told me that he had been throwing the ball and wasn't paying attention to how close he had gotten to the house and had busted his bedroom window. Well, this was a great opportunity to teach him. So, I told him you're not in trouble because you came and told me. Then I had him go help me fix the window. Oftentimes we mess up, and instead of running to our Father, we run from Him. We fear that He won't forgive us, but the opposite is true. You know that Jesus told the disciples that we should forgive seventy times seven in Matthew 18. Now if He requires this of us, isn't He going to require the same of Himself? Go to Jesus and ask for forgiveness and you will be forgiven.

1Jn 1:9 KJV If we confess our sins, he is faithful and just to forgive us our sins, and to cleanse us from all unrighteousness.

CXIII.

Have you ever really paid attention to cell towers out in a field? They have all these cables, called guy wires, anchoring them to the ground going every direction. These anchors run very deep. They are there to keep the tower from falling in the event of storms or high winds. Jesus is the anchor for our souls that keeps us from falling and being destroyed by the storms and winds of life. So, hold tight to the anchor and weather the storms.

Heb 6:19 NET We have this hope as an anchor for the soul, sure and steadfast, which reaches inside behind the curtain,

CXIV.

My little boy Isaac has this habit of asking why, why, why, and why. Sometimes I give him an explanation, but sometimes I tell him because. Sometimes he asks and I just look at him and he says "because?" I've heard people say don't ask God why. I'm not of the opinion that you can't ask God why. David and Job asked God why. Jesus was on the cross when He asked why. So, ask God why if you must. Just be satisfied if He just tells you because or if He doesn't tell you anything.

Isa 55:8-9 KJV 8 For my thoughts are not your thoughts, neither are your ways my ways, saith the LORD. 9 For as the heavens are higher than the earth, so are my ways higher than your ways, and my thoughts than your thoughts.

CXV.

Do you know what happens when you run your vehicle without oil or water? You'll blow up your engine. You can put all the gas in it you want, you can clean it, put the best sound system in it. Put some fancy lights in it, new carpet, etc. However, all of that doesn't matter if you've blown the engine. You see Jesus is our anointing oil and water, flowing through our lives. He is the oil that keeps us moving freely and the water that keeps our engine cool by giving us peace. You see many times we push on the gas in our spiritual lives. We go as fast as we can. We do as much as we can without being sure we are prayed up and full of Jesus. We dress right, put big lights in our churches, have the best sound system, and brand-new carpet. Are we full of Jesus, though? We can have all these things as long as we are full of Jesus and allow Him to flow through our lives. So, pray up and get full of Jesus, then worry about the rest.

Mat 25:2-4 KJV 2 And five of them were wise, and five were foolish. 3 They that were foolish took their lamps, and took no oil with them: 4 But the wise took oil in their vessels with their lamps.

CXVI.

What you're looking at here is a piece of coal. This piece of coal has been dug out of the ground and is now going to be used in one way or another to benefit others. It could be sent to a power plant where it will be crushed then burned to create power. This is done to provide electricity for countless numbers of people. Coal is also used to create activated carbon. Now. some of the uses in the list of things activated carbon is used for are astounding. A few of these things include sewage treatment, air purification, water purification, gold purification, medicine, and many other things. As you can see many times it is used to capture impurities. It may be that we are like this coal. We may not be the piece of coal that got turned into a diamond. Rather, we may be coal that is going through a different process. We may be helping to shine light into people's lives. We may be used in ministering to people and counseling them to get impurities out of their lives. We may even be like a medicine that helps bring healing into someone's life. We may just have a conversation over coffee to help others. Remember, nothing is insignificant in God's kingdom. Whatever we are being produced into, we must endure the process so that we may be used by God in a way to help others

"

Rom 9:21 NET Has the potter no right to make from the same lump of clay one vessel for special use and another for ordinary use?

Ecc 9:10 NET Whatever you find to do with your hands, do it with all your might.....

29 God's gifts and God's call are under full warranty - never canceled, never rescinded.

CXVII.

Do you know why toothpaste comes out when you squeeze a tube of toothpaste? Because that's what's in it. I'm sure you've injured yourself in some way before. Maybe you walked around the back of a truck and introduced your shin to the hitch. Or driving a nail in with a hammer and wham there's your finger. When this happens, we call this a Holy Ghost checker. It'll let you know what's in your heart. Because there's no time to think what's inside just comes out. I've heard many say Sweet Jesus, Oh Lord, or something like that when this happens. That's because that's what they are full of. Let's make sure that we are full of the right stuff. So, when we get squeezed by life, Jesus comes out.

Mat 12:34-35 KJV 34 O generation of vipers, how can ye, being evil, speak good things? for out of the abundance of the heart the mouth speaketh. 35 A good man out of the good treasure of the heart bringeth forth good things: and an evil man out of the evil treasure bringeth forth evil things.

CXVIII.

I once had a set of craftsman power tools that consisted of a sawzall, circular saw, light, and drill. Well, one day the battery pack quit working and the style battery and charger I needed were carried anymore. When I went to replace them, I ended up just buying a drill set with the charger. I took all the other tools and put them under my tool bench and kinda forgot about them. Four years later I was cleaning up in my shop and came across these tools. I begin to wonder if I ever even tried the new batteries on the old tools. I plugged the battery in one of the saws, and presto, it worked. I had an entire set of tools that I could have been using just sitting there. Some of us have tools that God has gifted us with that we could be utilizing. We may be working with part of our gift. Just like I was using part of my tool set, but not all of it. We may honestly think that we don't have the capability to use this gift anymore. Do what I did with the tool set. Try again, you may just find that your gift is sitting there waiting to be used.

1Pe 4:10 Easy English God has been good to each of you in different ways. He has given a gift to each of you, so that you are able to do certain things well. So, each of you should use your gift so that you can help other people. Then you will be God's good servants because you will be using his gifts properly.

Romans 11:29-36 MSG

29 God's gifts and God's call are under full warranty - never canceled, never rescinded.

CXIX.

When I was 19, I worked for a man doing manual labor. One particular day he had the crew at his house digging a septic tank hole by hand. One of the other workers and I had already gotten the hole pretty deep. So deep in fact that at 6'1" it was over my head. So, being the taller of the two, I was shoveling the dirt out. The other guy that was shorter was using a pickaxe to loosen the dirt. Once he got a good bit loose, I'd pitch it out of the hole. At some point I started daydreaming, waiting to shovel the next load out. As this happened some, let's say, intestinal gas found its way from my inside to the outside filling the hole that we were in. I had not even realized what had happened, not until the other worker just stopped in mid swing and turned and looked at me with disdain. This is the point that I began to laugh uncontrollably. He began to reprimand me, but the madder he got, the more I laughed. He started to try to get out of the hole, and I tried to assist. He just waved me away and said, "Don't touch me". He finally got out by himself, without my assistance. Though this is a funny story, let's take a different look. If we know someone who is down in a pit, which may even be of their own making and continual digging deeper and deeper, they need our help. So, we have to be attentive to those around us and not daydreaming like I was.

We don't need the stench of our lives or our negativity to engulf them. Also, we must be careful not to offend someone who is down. Because they really may need our help to get out of the pit, they are in. If we offend them, they may not accept our help. It may take them longer to get on level ground because of our actions. Let's stay focused and be a positive influence on those around us.

Eph 4:29 Easy English Be careful not to say anything that is bad. Say only good things that will help people. Then you will help to make them strong. You will help to give them what they need. And so, your words will be good for those who hear them.

Pro 18:19 KJV A brother offended is harder to be won than a strong city: and their contentions are like the bars of a castle.

CXX.

I had a friend once that was visiting some friends of his. While he was there, something happened to their cat that caused it to lose its life. They buried the cat. While the owners were standing there mourning the loss of their little cat, it dawned on my friend that he had a little toy in his pocket. When you pressed the button on it you would hear what sounded like somebody knocking on a door. Then a high-pitched voice that would say "Hey, hey let me out of here." Well, of course he pushed the button. At first a look of confusion came over them. Then everyone had a good laugh. You might think it was bad timing, but it did change the atmosphere. Sometimes in life you just gotta laugh. It could change the atmosphere around you. Laughter can help you through some tough situations. So, find something to laugh about.

Proverbs 17:22 NLT

22 A cheerful heart is good medicine,

but a broken spirit saps a person's strength.

CXXI.

I once knew a guy that at 19 years old was out late at night making some bad choices. These bad choices led him to the police picking him up. Once they got him to the station, they gave him a choice. They told him that he could call his dad to come pick him up or spend the night in jail. His response was "I'm not calling my daddy; I'll spend the night in jail." How many times have we heard if God loves people, he wouldn't let them go to hell? The thing is we have the same opportunity my friend did. We make bad decisions, then when given the opportunity to call on our Father we say no. Let's call on our heavenly Father today.

Isa 55:6-7 KJV 6 Seek ye the LORD while he may be found, call ye upon him while he is near: 7 Let the wicked forsake his way, and the unrighteous man his thoughts: and let him return unto the LORD, and he will have mercy upon him; and to our God, for he will abundantly pardon.

CXXII.

Uncle Fred was once in our local gas station when my daddy came in. They talked for a few minutes, and then my dad left. Now, daddy raised pigs and had a huge garden. He had been working all day tending to these, so he didn't smell like he'd been sitting under the air conditioner all day. A guy at the store made the following comment in Uncle Fred's ear shot. "I wish John would take a bath before he comes to the store." Now Uncle Fred didn't take this lightly. He told him, "You know what, he may be dirty on the outside, but you're dirty on the inside, and I'd much rather be around him than you." Too often folks are quick to comment like the man in this story talking about my daddy. They don't take into account what harm their words could do. We ought not be saying hurtful things anyway, but words that are helpful, encouraging and kind.

Eph 4:32 NET Instead, be kind to one another, compassionate, forgiving one another, just as God in Christ also forgave you.

CXXIII.

We've all most likely heard the phrase "try this, it'll change your life." It may have been a food or experience. It might have been their favorite vacation spot or favorite restaurant. Whatever it is people believe that it is a life changing experience. Well, the fact is, Jesus really is a life changing experience. Not only this life, but the one to come. So, while you're out there experiencing life, you should try Jesus because He really will change your life.

Psa 34:8 KJV O taste and see that the LORD is good: blessed is the man that trusteth in him.

CXXIV.

I had brought my little boy Isaac to the park. As we were walking in, he was walking towards the park and looking back at his sister while walking forward. Obviously, he started veering off, and I had to turn him around so he would look where he was going. Just like Isaac, we too, get distracted sometimes by what is behind us. This can cause us to veer off the path God has for us. If it's in the past, leave it there and keep walking towards Jesus.

Pro 4:25 BBE Keep your eyes on what is in front of you, looking straight before you.

CXXV.

My wife, Kristina, and I were walking around in our pasture with our little boy. We were constantly changing his direction because of ant beds, thistles or anything that could be a threat. He didn't see the threats; he was just walking. Often God may change our direction in life. It may be a delay in traffic, a relationship that doesn't work out, a job loss, or whatever. We don't understand why, but He is watching out for us. We just have to trust that he knows best and wants the best for us.

Psa 32:8 KJV I will instruct thee and teach thee in the way which thou shalt go: I will guide thee with mine eye.

Jer 29:11 KJV For I know the thoughts that I think toward you, saith the LORD, thoughts of peace, and not of evil, to give you an expected end.

CXXVI.

I was recently on a playground that I had grown up playing on. There was a brick wall there that used to be so huge. We would try to climb it, or we would go up behind it where the hill went right up to the top of it. I walked over to it to check it out and realized that it was just over 3 feet. The wall was never very big; I just needed to grow up to see that. We often run into brick walls in our spiritual lives, and at the time we think they are so huge. Once we get past them, however, we are able to look back and realize that they weren't so big after all. We just had to grow.

2Pe 3:18 KJV But grow in grace, and in the knowledge of our Lord and Saviour Jesus Christ. To him be glory both now and forever. Amen.

Eph 4:15 KJV But speaking the truth in love, may grow up into him in all things, which is the head, even Christ:

CXXVII.

Every morning we get up from our warm beds in our warm houses, and we may go grab a cup of coffee and some breakfast if we choose. Then we go get in our vehicles and drive to our jobs. The whole time we are complaining, I didn't get enough sleep, it's too early, I wish I didn't have to work. In the meanwhile, there are people that slept in the cold last night with no supper, no warm house, no choice of breakfast, no vehicle, no job to go to. Sometimes we need to be reminded of how blessed we are. The children of Israel complained in the wilderness and a generation died there. Don't die in the wilderness, be thankful.

1 Thessalonians 5:18 KJV In every thing give thanks: for this is the will of God in Christ Jesus concerning you.

CXXVIII.

I was at a company picnic, and there were a lot of games going on for the kids. My oldest son Joshua, probably 11 at the time, signed up for this race. The winner won a fishing pole. Boy, was he excited! Now some of the other kids in the race were much older and subsequently taller. That being said, I knew my son wasn't going to win this race. He ran as hard as he could, but the older kids were faster. I could see the disappointment on his face as the others crossed the finish line before him. I immediately went to him. I told him he had no reason to be upset. He did his best, and that's all that mattered. Now, for those of you that feel bad for him, the lady in charge of the games stepped in after I had my conversation with him. She told him she had another game for a fishing pole. She then told him to guess a number between 1 and 10. I don't remember what number he called, but it didn't matter if he would have said 15. When he told her his number, she said that's it, you win the other pole. The takeaway here is. Run the race. You can't compare yourself to others. They may be older in the kingdom and have years of experience and exercising their faith. They may be well ahead of you. Also, don't compare yourself to others that may have started the race when you did. They may have a different ministry than you, and it may look like they are well ahead of you. You run your race. Your race may be different, but it's yours. Your ministry may be different, but it's yours. Do the best you can, run your race, and remember we all win in the end if we finish.

Heb 12:1 KJV Wherefore seeing we also are compassed about with so great a cloud of witnesses, let us lay aside every weight, and the sin which doth so easily beset us, and let us run with patience the race that is set before us,

Rev 3:11 ISV I am coming soon! Hold on to what you have so that no one takes your victor's crown.

CXXIX.

I was working with some other guys on a silo. We were way up in the air on a catwalk and were taking turns going in the silo to work. Another guy and I were standing outside the silo waiting for our turn when, suddenly, a dragonfly came flying up. The other guy, who was probably 6'5", saw it flying up and started going into a panic. He started backing up into me saying "it's a horse fly" repeatedly. I grabbed the back of his shirt and pushed him forward gently. I then told him that it was a dragonfly and would not harm him. I added though even if it were, you'd be better to be stung by it than fall from up here. The thing is, he could have reached out and clapped his hands on it and eliminated what he saw as a threat. Too often, when we see what we perceive as a threat, we panic first. Then, if we aren't careful, we can cause more damage trying to dodge the "threat" than facing it head on. God, or someone else that God uses, then has to get ahold of us and get us straightened out so we face what is before us. Do you know that the phrase "do not fear" is in the Bible 365 times? Hmm, that seems awfully coincidental, but there aren't any coincidences with God. So, let's not fear, but trust that God is going to take care of us.

Isa 41:10 ISV Don't be afraid, because I'm with you; don't be anxious, because I am your God. I keep on strengthening you; I'm truly helping you. I'm surely upholding you with my victorious right hand."

CXXX.

My daughter Hannah was a preemie baby when she was born. God did a miraculous work in her though because she had no issues. If you weren't told, you wouldn't have known that she was a preemie. After she was home for some time, the hospital reached out. They sent a nurse to my house to tell me that they wanted to come work with her on physical therapy. I told the nurse that there was nothing wrong with her. I told her that God had healed her. She insisted that they come work with her. I told her that it was fine if they worked with her, but it was a waste of time. After 2 months of working with her the nurse said, "You know there isn't anything wrong with this baby." I told her that I had tried to tell her that 2 months prior. You see I was absolutely convinced that there wasn't anything wrong with Hannah. Let's look at what the Bible says about Abraham's faith.

Rom 4:18-24 ISV 18 Hoping in spite of hopeless circumstances, he believed that he would become "the father of many nations," just as he had been told: "This is how many descendants you will have." 19 His faith did not weaken when he thought about his own body (which was already as good as dead now that he was about a hundred years old) or about Sarah's inability to have children, 20 nor did he doubt God's promise out of a lack of faith. Instead, his faith became stronger and he gave glory to God, 21 being absolutely convinced that God would do what he had promised. 22 This is why "it was credited to him as righteousness." 23 Now the words "it was credited to him" were written not only for him 24 but also for us. Our faith will be regarded in the same way, if we believe in the one who raised Jesus our Lord from the dead.

He hoped in spite of hopelessness. His faith did not weaken. He didn't doubt God's promise, instead his faith became stronger. He was absolutely convinced that God would do what He said He would. And our faith can be the same. There are things about God, that if challenged, we would not accept anything other than what we believe. We believe Jesus came to die for our sins, we believe He was resurrected, and we believe that He is coming back. Yet, we worry if He will take care of us. Will He heal? Will He provide? Will He forgive me again? I want so badly for us as a whole to have a revival of faith in God. I want us to have faith like Abraham and be absolutely convinced.

Rom 10:17 KJV So then faith cometh by hearing, and hearing by the word of God.

CXXXI.

I once was cleaning up under a machine at a previous job. I had all my PPE (personal protective equipment) including my hard hat. I finished up, and I was coming from under the machine when I ran right into a metal pipe. I hit it so hard it knocked my hard hat off. I shook it off and went on with what I had to do. Had I not been wearing my hard hat, I could have been injured badly. There's a lot of different PPE out there that is intended to protect you from harm. Some may be immediate harm and some you don't feel for a while like hearing loss. Either way, if you don't use it, it won't help. We have PPE in the kingdom of God as well. It's called the Armor of God. It's there to protect us. However, if we don't wear it, it won't help. So, let's put on our Armor.

Eph 6:10-17 KJV 10 Finally, my brethren, be strong in the Lord, and in the power of his might. 11 Put on the whole armour of God, that ye may be able to stand against the wiles of the devil. 12 For we wrestle not against flesh and blood, but against principalities, against powers, against the rulers of the darkness of this world, against spiritual wickedness in high places. 13 Wherefore take unto you the whole armour of God, that ye may be able to withstand in the evil day, and having done all, to stand. 14 Stand therefore, having your loins girt about with truth, and having on the breastplate of righteousness; 15 And your feet shod with the preparation of the gospel of peace; 16 Above all, taking the shield of faith, wherewith ye shall be able to quench all the fiery darts of the wicked. 17 And take the helmet of salvation, and the sword of the Spirit, which is the word of God:

CXXXII.

Have you ever been driving and notice a blemish on your windshield? Or maybe you are watching TV and see a spot on your screen. After you see it, that's all you can focus on. You try to ignore it, but it just keeps getting in your line of sight. Sometimes, we may see a blemish in someone. It might be a character flaw; it might be something they are doing wrong. It may actually just be that they are different from you. Did you know that we are all different and at some point, we will not agree on something? Here's the thing, though. Don't let the blemish that you see distort how you see the person. You pray for them, and you love them. If they ask for your help to remove that blemish, then you help them. Just don't look down on them.

Gal 6:1-2 WEB 1 Brothers, even if a man is caught in some fault, you who are spiritual must restore such a one in a spirit of gentleness; looking to yourself so that you also aren't tempted. 2 Bear one another's burdens, and so fulfill the law of Christ.

1Jn 4:20 KJV If a man say, I love God, and hateth his brother, he is a liar: for he that loveth not his brother whom he hath seen, how can he love God whom he hath not seen?

CXXXIII.

My daddy told me a story about this young boy that was getting beat up by this other boy every day after school. This went on for some time. One day when the young boy made it home his daddy told him that if he let that boy whoop him again, he'd get another whooping when he got home. Well, the young boy wasn't interested in that. The next day the bully shows up like clockwork. He asks, "You ready for your whooping?" To this the young boy replied, "I guess, but do you mind if I get a dip of snuff first?" The bully says, "Fine with me." The young boy asks, "Do you want a dip?" The bully answers, "No." The young boy then says, "Have one anyway," and dashes powdered snuff in the bully's eyes. He then commences to whooping the bully right good. From that point the bully never messed with him again. The enemy tries to bully us and will make a pattern if we allow him to. He'll keep attacking at a weak point. Remember when we are weak, He is strong. It may not even seem like big things. It may be a stomachache, headache, or some other discomfort that comes around when it's time for a church service. Any device meant to keep you from Jesus is a tactic of the bully, keeping you from the very thing you need. It must be fought against and not indulged. He will push us around and try to make us do his bidding. What we need to do is be like this boy. No, we don't throw snuff in his eyes (though sometimes it may be tempting). No, the weapons of our warfare are not carnal, but they are mighty. So, let's arm ourselves with the weapons that God gives us and defeat the enemy.

Jas 4:7 KJV Submit yourselves therefore to God. Resist the devil, and he will flee from you.

2Co 10:4-5 KJV 4 (For the weapons of our warfare are not carnal, but mighty through God to the pulling down of strong holds;) 5 Casting down imaginations, and every high thing that exalteth itself against the knowledge of God, and bringing into captivity every thought to the obedience of Christ;

CXXXIV.

Once, when I was quite a bit younger, I had gotten angry about something that probably didn't amount to a hill of beans. I was steaming. I was moving angry, you know fast, without any care of what was going on around me. I was fixing to hop in my truck and then drive angry. I went to get in my truck, and I hit my head so hard it knocked me back a step. Immediately I said, "Okay, Lord, I got it. You don't have to hit me again." Don't be like I was and get in the position where God has to knock you upside the head to get your attention. Sometimes we get wrapped up in ourselves and forget that we need to be Christ-like. Let's be sensitive to the Spirit and make sure we are portraying attributes that honor Jesus.

Psa 119:67 ISV Before I was humbled, I wandered away, but now I observe your words.

Psa 119:71 ISV It was for my good that I was humbled; so that I would learn your statutes.

CXXXV.

When I was in my early twenties and young in the Lord, my daddy came down very sick. He was 80 years old at the time. I prayed and prayed for him to get better. At some point in the process, I felt like God had let me know that he would be okay. I received a couple different conformations on that as well. Shortly thereafter, my daddy passed away. Boy that took a toll on me. Not only had I lost my daddy, which was enough in itself, but I had also been given this promise by God that he'd be okay. I struggled with this for some time. Did I really hear from God? If so, what's going on? Did God abandon me? The questions loomed as I mourned the loss of my daddy. The thing is, God impressed me that he'd be okay, and I interpreted that the way I saw it. Because okay to me was that he would get better. God doesn't see things the same way we do. His ways are higher than our ways, and His thoughts higher than ours. It finally hit me that when God said he'd be okay that meant he'd be okay with God. I do believe God was letting me know that my daddy would make heaven, which is a greater healing. So, if you've lost a loved one or some situation didn't work out like you thought it would, know that God has not forsaken you. Am I telling you that you won't be hurt, or you won't face disappointment? No, I'm not. What I am telling you is that God can heal your heart. Don't walk away from God because you're hurt. He's the only one that can heal your hurt anyway. Instead draw closer to Him, and he may make things clearer to you. If not, then when you don't understand God, trust Him.

Pro 3:5 KJV Trust in the LORD with all thine heart; and lean not unto thine own understanding.

Psa 147:3 KJV He healeth the broken in heart, and bindeth up their wounds.

CXXXVI.

If you're a coffee drinker, then your coffee cup cabinet probably looks like ours. We've got so many different kinds of coffee cups and tumblers it's a little ridiculous. It works for us though. If someone comes over, it's easy for them to grab a cup that fits them and enjoy their coffee. The church is like a coffee cup cabinet. Made up of people that are different. They come from different backgrounds and have different experiences. It sometimes may look ridiculous how all these people fit together, but it works. We are all different so we can reach different people. There are some people that only you can reach. There are some that only your neighbor can reach. We all can take what is good and give it to people so their lives can be filled with Jesus. Let's strive to be a good vessel for the Master's use.

2Ti 2:21 WEB If anyone therefore purges himself from these, he will be a vessel for honor, sanctified, and suitable for the master's use, prepared for every good work.

Joh 4:13-14 KJV 13 Jesus answered and said unto her, Whosoever drinketh of this water shall thirst again: 14 But whosoever drinketh of the water that I shall give him shall never thirst; but the water that I shall give him shall be in him a well of water springing up into everlasting life.

CXXXVII.

Dad. That's a little word for everything that comes with it. As dads we are providers, protectors, comforters, instructors, teachers, disciplinarians, etc. We've got a lot of hats to wear as do moms. We as dads have something that is not often thought of. We more than often put the belief in our children of what God is like. I'm not saying that we portray God-like qualities, though we should. I'm saying how we act with them is how they will likely see God. Now, hopefully, they will grow to see God truly as He is. At first, children and even adults that first come to God put our attributes of how we see dads on God, because he is our heavenly Father. If an adult comes in that had an overbearing or abusive dad, it's going to be hard for them to trust God. If all we ever do is fuss, then they will just be waiting for God to be the same way when they mess up. I know we have to discipline, but everything we do should be in love. We are imprinting on our children's brains the way they will see God. What do you want them to see? Let's do what we do as dads, but let's do it in a way that God will be glorified.

Just a side note. Do you think it was a coincidence that verse 12 the "golden rule" follows the scriptures talking about being a father/dad? Think about it.

Mat 7:9-12 WEB 9 Or who is there among you who, if his son asks him for bread, will give him a stone? 10 Or if he asks for a fish, who will give him a serpent? 11 If you then, being evil, know how to give good gifts to your children, how much more will your Father who is in heaven give good things to those who ask him! 12 Therefore, whatever you desire for men to do to you, you shall also do to them; for this is the law and the prophets.

Eph 6:4 KJV And, ye fathers, provoke not your children to wrath: but bring them up in the nurture and admonition of the Lord

CXXXVIII.

I've seen it many times over, a bride planning her wedding and getting so immersed in every detail. I've seen them get so stressed that they were about to explode. The problem is, they get so wrapped up in what they are doing that they forget why they are doing it. They've forgotten that there is a man that they feel in love with that they want to spend the rest of their lives with. We have to be careful because we can fall into this same trap. We can get too wrapped up in what we are doing for the kingdom. We want every single detail to work just right. Not saying that we shouldn't give it our best, but we get to working on this and working on that, and before you know it, we're doing like Martha. We're busy working that we've forgotten about our first love, Jesus. Isn't it interesting in Revelations 2 that when addressing the church in Ephesus that the first thing mentioned is their work? Then it's shortly followed by 'Rev 2:4 KJV Nevertheless I have somewhat against thee, because thou hast left thy first love.' Let's make sure we are focusing on our relationship with Jesus more than what we are doing for Him.

Luke 10:40-42 ISV 40 But Martha was worrying about all the things she had to do, so she came to him and asked, "Lord, you do care that my sister has left me to do the work all by myself, don't you? Then tell her to help me." 41 The Lord answered her, "Martha, Martha! You worry and fuss about a lot of things. 42 But there's only one thing you need. Mary has chosen what is better, and it is not to be taken away from her."

CXXXIX.

I want to be more like you, Jesus. How many of us have prayed that prayer? We want to shine His light unto the world. We want to reflect God's glory. Well, go with me for a minute. In Ezekiel 28, the Bible talks about the devil. It describes the stones that were in him. Interestingly enough in Exodus 28, the stones of the priest's breastplate are listed.

Eze 28:13 KJV the sardius, topaz, and the diamond, the beryl, the onyx, and the jasper, the sapphire, the emerald, and the carbuncle, and gold

Exo 28:17-20 KJV 17 a sardius, a topaz, and a carbuncle, an emerald, a sapphire, and a diamond, a ligure, an agate, and an amethyst, a beryl, and an onyx, and a jasper: they shall be set in gold in their inclosings.

Now we know that the devils original design was meant to reflect God's glory. Imagine if you will, God entering the "anointed cherub's" presence and God's light shining against all those stones. This must have been a beautiful sight to behold. Apparently, this went to the devil's head, and well, we know the rest of the story. Now, let's pay attention that there are three stones in the priest's breastplate that were not in the devil's design. These three are the ligure, the agate and the amethyst. I would like to focus on the color of these three. Because if you're trying to reflect light, color matters. The ligure is a yellowish green color. The agate is blue, red, purple, black, green, brown, pink. The amethyst is purple. I find it interesting that bruises can be blue, purple, black, pink, brown, or yellow green. Follow me if you will. This is how we differ from the enemy. We have the ability to know Jesus on a different level. We can be like Him through suffering. We may suffer with Him and for Him. If you're having trouble or pain, rejoice. Yes, rejoice that we get to have this fellowship that the angels who are in His presence cannot. With all that being said, know that if we are going to be more like Jesus and shine His light. Then we most likely will go through suffering but understand that it is not that God has forgotten us. No, it is that He is making us more like Him.

Phi 3:10 KJV That I may know him, and the power of his resurrection, and the fellowship of his sufferings, being made conformable unto his death;

Phi 3:10 Easy English The only thing that I want is to know Christ. He rose, to become alive again, after he had died. And I want to know in myself how powerful his new life is. Also, I want to have troubles and pain, as he did. I want to become like him in his death.

Rom 5:3-5 WEB 3 Not only this, but we also rejoice in our sufferings, knowing that suffering produces perseverance; 4 and perseverance, proven character; and proven character, hope: 5 and hope doesn't disappoint us, because God's love has been poured into our hearts through the Holy Spirit who was given to us.

CXL.

Imagine, if you will, that your house caught on fire, and you rushed to get your stuff out, but you had children in the house. Someone else runs in and saves your kids that you left behind. Now, obviously, this sounds absurd. As parents, the first thing we would do is get our children out before we even thought about our stuff. Yet there are many parents walking around so concerned about their lives, their activities, their wants, and their stuff that they have not focused on getting their children to God. They miss church over any little thing. They bad mouth their brothers and sisters in the church, including the pastor. They don't make the kingdom of God a priority because it would interfere with their stuff. All the while they are putting their children on a path that leads to everlasting fire. Hopefully, if the parents won't change, someone else steps in and saves them before it's too late, but the responsibility lies with the parents first and foremost. We need to be very attentive to our children's salvation. Noah had this testimony, that he saved his family from God's wrath. We need to be soul winners at home first and strive to save our children.

Mat 19:14 ISV Jesus, however, said, "Let the little children come to me, and stop keeping them away, because the kingdom from heaven belongs to people like these."

Deu 5:29 ISV If only they would commit to fear me and keep all my commands, then it will go well with them and their children forever.

CXLI.

One day we brought our 3-year-old, Isaac, to the zoo. Boy, he had a good time. He rode a train, saw all kinds of animals, and got to feed the fish. He was so excited. As we were walking towards the exit he tripped and scraped his elbow pretty good. It wasn't stitch worthy, but it definitely needed a band-aid and some antiseptic. He was crying as we were trying to comfort him. Finally, we got him cleaned up and taken care of. The rest of the day all he wanted to talk about was his "boo-boo." The next day he was telling the same story. He wasn't talking about all the animals that he saw, the train ride, or the fun he had. Nope, he had forgotten all the fun and was fixated on the bad that happened. We often do the same thing. We may be having a great day when one little thing happens that upsets us, and that's all we focus on. As I've heard before, there are 86,400 seconds in a day, don't let a few seconds out of the day ruin the rest of it. Let's choose to be more positive, focusing on the good.

Eph 4:29 Easy English Be careful not to say anything that is bad. Say only good things that will help people. Then you will help to make them strong. You will help to give them what they need. And so, your words will be good for those who hear them.

Psa 19:14 KJV Let the words of my mouth, and the meditation of my heart, be acceptable in thy sight, O LORD, my strength, and my redeemer.

CXLII.

I'm dying, you're dying, a loved one is dying. Words that no one wants to hear. All the "what if's" and "why's" roll through our heads. At some point a thought will arise. Am I/they right with God? The fact of the matter is, we are all dying every day. Every day we get a little closer to our last day. We should continually ask ourselves if we are right with God because we never know when our last day will be. So, we should live our lives every day like it could be our last.

Matthew 24:43-44 KJV 43 But know this, that if the goodman of the house had known in what watch the thief would come, he would have watched, and would not have suffered his house to be broken up. 44 Therefore be ye also ready: for in such an hour as ye think not the Son of man cometh.

CXLIII.

Remember the toys that we had as kids that you had to put the right shape in the right hole? It didn't matter how hard you tried, you had to put the star shape in the star hole and square shape in the square hole. That's the way it works. Too many times as adults we try to fit in places we aren't meant to. What do I mean? Well, I'm glad you asked. I'm sure you've heard someone tell a young man, "You ought to be a preacher." Or a young woman, "you ought to be a teacher or a singer." They may be right, but they may not be. If you pour all your effort into being something that you're not called to be, you'll burn out quickly. This may even result in you backsliding and quitting on God entirely. You may not have a glorious calling. You may be called to help people. You know, that is a calling. In 1 Corinthians 12:28 it's talking about apostles, prophets, teachers, miracle workers, then it jumps in with helps and governments. One translation says those people who are able to help other people and those people who are guides to other people. One calling is no more important than another. What is important is that you are in your calling. So, make sure that you are in your calling so that you can fulfill your purpose and not burn out. It doesn't matter if you are called to clean toilets or preach a message, do it all for the glory of God.

2Pe 1:10 KJV Wherefore the rather, brethren, give diligence to make your calling and election sure: for if ye do these things, ye shall never fall:

1Co 10:31 KJV Whether therefore ye eat, or drink, or whatsoever ye do, do all to the glory of God.

CXLIV.

I had a tree in my yard that I cut down. After sitting there, a couple weeks I decided to move it. Once I got to it, I noticed it had green leaves on it. Against all odds the tree was producing. We should be like this tree. It doesn't matter if we've been knocked down, if we don't have the connections we used to. Nor should it matter if someone is telling us you're dead and useless. We should produce anyway. There was a story in the 2 Kings 13 where a dead man was thrown into Elisha's sepulcher, and when the man touched Elisha's bones he was brought back to life. We may not be physically dead, but we may feel dead. We may feel useless and not needed. Let's move past feelings and live for God anyway. Let's reach those that are lost anyway, let's do the right thing anyway and let's strive to produce against all odds.

1Pe 3:15 WEB But sanctify the Lord God in your hearts. Always be ready to give an answer to everyone who asks you a reason concerning the hope that is in you, with humility and fear,

2Ti 4:2 KJV Preach the word; be instant in season, out of season; reprove, rebuke, exhort with all longsuffering and doctrine.

CXLV.

You know there are things we grew up with that our children may have no idea about. They may not know how to write checks, or use a rotary phone, or go outside and turn the antenna so we can watch the TV. Soon, daylight savings time changes will stop from what I've been told. If it does, what we've known our entire lives will be a foreign concept to new generations. Just think about trying to explain that to children one day, how absurd it will sound. These things may be trivial and don't really matter much. What does matter though, is that we must make sure that our children and generations to come know about Jesus and the things of God. We cannot let these things be forgotten. We must make every effort to teach and instruct others in the ways of God.

Deu 6:7-9 WEB 7 and you shall teach them diligently to your children and shall talk of them when you sit in your house, and when you walk by the way, and when you lie down, and when you rise up. 8 You shall bind them for a sign on your hand, and they shall be for frontlets between your eyes. 9 You shall write them on the door posts of your house and on your gates.

CXLVI.

I saw a house one day that had a dual staircase that swayed out away from each other then back in at the top. There was a nice corvette sitting out front. Someone said that's how you know you've made it. Now, I'm not saying that I'm against having nice things, but having nice things is not a good indicator to know you've made it. These things are only temporary and will one day be nonexistent. You've made it when you are at home in the presence of God. You've made it when your family desires to live for God. You've really made it when you finally get to see Jesus in heaven. So, let's strive to be like Abraham who looked for a city whose builder and maker was God. So, we can say, now I've made it.

Heb 11:10 KJV For he looked for a city which hath foundations, whose builder and maker is God.

CXLVII.

Imagine that you're a business owner. A friend of yours has broken the law and landed themselves in jail. Not only are they in jail, but they are going to be there a long time. Plus, they can't afford to bail themselves out because bail is too high. So out of the kindness of your heart you decide to not only bail them out but give them a job too. After a short time, they begin to be hit and miss about coming to work. When you run into them outside of work, they don't seem to want to talk to you. You've even noticed them avoiding you and pretending they didn't hear or see you. So, one day when they do show up for work you stop them and ask why. Why are they missing work and why are they avoiding you? They answer with, "Well, I think I deserve more. More pay, more benefits, more time off so I can do what I want. Plus, I don't like some of these other workers here, and honestly, I don't like this job." Could you imagine the audacity of someone doing this? Or could you imagine how you would feel as the business owner? The truth of the matter is Jesus paid a debt that we could not pay. We were doomed for eternity, and He paid to set us free. Then He gives us a new life where we get to live for Him. Yes, I said get to not have to. Yet people will give the lamest excuses to not attend church or live for Jesus on a day-to-day basis. They deserve more, they don't like the people, they are too busy, etc. We should not be making excuses to not go to church or live for God. Instead, we should make excuses to always live for God and faithfully attend church. We don't honestly need an excuse because we have the reason- Jesus!

1Co 6:19-20 KJV 19 What? know ye not that your body is the temple of the Holy Ghost which is in you, which ye have of God, and ye are not your own? 20 For ye are bought with a price: therefore glorify God in your body, and in your spirit, which are God's.

CXLVIII.

I had a friend once tell me the story about a very wealthy man and wife that he had gone to eat with. Now, I'll mention that the wealthy man was a humble man. As they were sitting there the wife asked do you think I could get a steak. To which he replied with a hmm, I guess. My friend piped up YOU GUESS? He said you could buy the restaurant and you guess. The rich man had a poor man's mentality. He just didn't understand how much money he had. It makes me think of the phrase "All we can do is pray." How many times have we said or heard that? I know most of the time this is probably said in a situation where we can't do anything in our power to fix whatever is wrong. We try to comfort someone or ourselves with this phrase. We, like the rich man, do not understand what we have. The power of prayer has raised the dead, healed the sick, saved the lost, and set free the captives. It's what we were made to do, to communicate with God. It's not "all we can do," it's the most important thing we can do. So, let's not underestimate the power that we have access to in prayer.

1Ti 2:1 KJV I exhort therefore, that, first of all, supplications, prayers, intercessions, and giving of thanks, be made for all men;

CXLIX.

I was riding with my oldest son one day when he was just a little boy. He turns to me and asks "Daddy, do you make Jesus happy?" To which I replied, "Well, son, I try. I hope so." He then says, "I make Jesus happy." I say, "You do? How do you do that?" What he said next stunned me. "Because I'm happy." What a profound thought to hear from a child, but oh so true. We need not spend our lives unhappy but be happy in the Lord. Thus, we will make Him happy.

Phi 4:4 Easy English Always be happy because you live united to the Lord. I will say it again, 'Be happy!'

CL.

My grandpa, whose real name was Ernest, was known to most folks by the nickname "Bull Ballard." Most thought he got this name because of his strength. My daddy told me the real reason. Grandpa was working with a crew of men one day, and one of them told the others that he had a picture of Grandpa holding two bulls by the head. They bantered back and forth about it until finally he told them he'd bring the picture the next day. When the others walked away my grandpa asked the man why he said that, because he knew that he didn't have a picture of him. The man replied, "Trust me, be here tomorrow and you'll see." The next day the man arrived with a picture (this would have been an old, unclear black and white photo) of what looked like my grandpa holding two bulls by the head. From that point on he was called Bull Ballard. To Grandpa this was impossible, but the man wanted him to just believe him. We read over and over in the Word about faith and believing. Jesus tells us everything is possible if we believe. So, let's start believing.

Mar 9:23 ISV Jesus told him, "'If you are able?' Everything is possible for the person who believes!"

CLI.

There was a story told about a Pastor that was in the pulpit preaching a sermon. As he was preaching, he asked "Who all here wants to go to heaven?" Every hand in the place popped up except for one old man in the back. Noticing this the Pastor circled his sermon back around to the same question, but with a little more fervency this time. Still the old man just sat there. Puzzled and concerned at this point he made his way back to the same question with all the zeal that he could muster up. Still the old man just sat there. The Pastor finished his sermon, then hurriedly made his way to the man. He approached him and began to address the old man. He said, "I noticed that when I asked who all wanted to go to heaven, you didn't raise your hand." The old man replied, "No, sir, I'm not interested in that." The Pastor said, "You mean when you die you don't want to go to heaven?" The old man says, "That's a different story. I thought you were gathering a load to go right now." This is a funny story, but I wanted to use it to illustrate something. We should always be prepared because we do not know when our time may come. So be ready because we won't have a choice to go or not.

Mat 24:44 KJV Therefore be ye also ready: for in such an hour as ye think not the Son of man cometh.

CLII.

Let's say you built a house. You get everything designed and built just like you wanted. You live in this house for some time. Then, one day, you decide I need to paint this room, or knock out that wall and add another room, or remodel the bathroom. Just because you built it just like you wanted, doesn't mean there won't be changes that have to happen. God is the God of all creation. He literally created everything. We believe this, but we look at that as past tense. Why would the psalmist say Create in me a clean heart oh Lord, if He was done with creating? We come and go from the presence of the creator and never change. We aren't letting Him create in us what He wants.

He wants to renew our mind (Romans 12:2), He wants to put His law in our hearts and our minds (Jeremiah 31:33, Hebrews 10:16), He wants to create in us a clean heart and a right spirit. (Psalm 51:10). So let us come open before our creator to become what He would have us be.

Psa 127:1 KJV Except the LORD build the house, they labour in vain that build it...

CLIII. One Last Thing

There are two types of coffee drinkers. There are those that will drink it if it's made, and there are those that will make it if it ain't. Now, you may not drink coffee, but this can still apply to you. Just like with the coffee, there are those that will drink up the Spirit of God when He moves. They are satisfied with experiencing God in weekly church services. Then there are those that hunger and thirst after God daily. They want to commune with God and want God to be a part of their everyday life. So, they make a relationship with God a daily priority. They will make it happen, not just enjoy it if it happens. Be intentional and make it happen.

If this book has helped you deepen your walk with God, and you would like more devotionals like these, visit our website GroundedandSettled.net.

CLIV. Copyrights

Throughout this devotional, scriptures from multiple versions of the Bible.

New Living Translation

Scripture quotations marked (NLT) are taken from the Holy Bible, New Living Translation, copyright ©1996, 2004, 2015 by Tyndale House Foundation. Used by permission of Tyndale House Publishers, Carol Stream, Illinois 60188. All rights reserved.

International Standard Version

Scripture taken from the Holy Bible: International Standard Version® Release 2.0. Copyright © 1996-2013 by the ISV Foundation. Used by permission of Davidson Press, LLC. ALL RIGHTS RESERVED INTERNATIONALLY.

Easy English

Scripture quotations are from the Easy English Bible Copyright © MissionAssist 2019 - Charitable Incorporated Organization 1162807. Used by permission. All rights reserved."

New English Translation

The Scriptures quoted are from the NET Bible® https://netbible.com[1] copyright ©1996, 2019 used with permission from Biblical Studies Press, L.L.C. All rights reserved".

The Message

Scripture quotations marked MSG are taken from The Message, copyright © 1993, 2002, 2018 by Eugene H. Peterson. Used by permission of NavPress. All rights reserved. Represented by Tyndale House Publishers.

---

1.   https://netbible.com/